We're all in this together.

For Johnny,
Mom and Dad,
Deb, Dale, Jenny
and Captain.

Thank you for making this Journey with me,
For always, supporting my work,
even when you thought I was
just being an old hippie!
For accepting me for who I am,
For teaching me a strong work ethic,
For showing me that family is always first,
For teaching me that LOVE always
brings me home and that I will always
have a home with you,
For always making me feel safe,
For being a family that lives by the
Golden Rule and for

EMBRACING THE CONTRAST.

You are my heroes.
J

APPRECIATION
A NOTE FROM THE AUTHOR

When I was a little girl, I was so connected. To the trees, to the sky, to my family, to animals, to God. There was no doubt in my mind that life was beautiful and amazing. I knew it when I rode my pony, went sled riding in our backyard, rolled down the hill landing in a pile of leaves, and as I walked through the forest to visit my grandmother. I am so connected to all of this, I thought to myself. I could feel the trees breathing. God is good. I just knew it.

Then I grew up and while my heart held these beliefs close, I began unlearning these powerful truths. I started to pay attention to what other people said, thought and believed. It became important to me although I really didn't understand why. No one told me it mattered, it just seemed like it should. To be honest, I didn't really like people that much. I liked animals. They were much easier to talk to and always loved me unconditionally even when I lost patience with them. I couldn't say the same about people.

MY STORY has taken many turns, as I'm sure yours has as well. It's been amazing, horrible, fantastic, and miserable. It's been painful, lonely, and full of love, and it has come full circle. I have finally reconnected. I remember who I am: a little girl just figuring it out and trying to have as much fun as possible. I've found that my patterns of behavior have created beliefs, some have served me; some not so much. But it's good to understand what you don't want or like as it brings you closer to knowing what *feels* right. I truly believe that the Universe loves me and knows my heart. I believe this to be true for each of us.

MY STORY

VOLUME I

Written by Jani Roberts
Edited by Sabrina Ursaner

© 2021 Alignment Essentials, LLC. All rights reserved.

Illustrations by Michelle Hays, Joyce Weller, and various artists.

I know that I have not made mistakes nor has anyone else (this can be a hard truth to swallow cause then who ya gonna blame?) but I believe each of us is doing the best that we can with the tools that we are aware of.

Each day I build new beliefs, change patterns and find new ways of thinking. I care less about what others think and more about how I feel. I remember to mind my own business and always try to treat others as I would like to be treated. This is my promise. And when my feet get stuck in the mud, I'll do what I need to do. Even if it means leaving the shoes behind.

Each day I will work the practice. I will quiet my mind. I will listen. I'll try.

Now this is YOUR STORY. Let YOUR STORY be your path to follow, to build, to reconnect, to find your way. You've made no mistakes. Have as much fun as possible and always remember, we are in this together.

In appreciation,
J

Welcome to your story.

The one you have written and the one you shall write. As you create your own experience on the pages that follow, we ask you to remember that you cannot get it wrong and you will never get it done.

Be easy about this process.

In appreciation,
Jani

Warriors
These are powerful souls
Spiritual in nature
They are driven by strength,
determination and love
They gain their strength
Through the empowerment of others
Their work is their food.

How to create my daily experience:

Patterns of Behavior:

THOUGHTS CREATE BELIEFS. BELIEFS CREATE PATTERNS OF BEHAVIOR. PATTERNS OF BEHAVIORS CREATE OUR REALITY. THEREFORE, WHAT WE ARE EXPERIENCING IS SIMPLY A RESULT OF OUR THOUGHTS. WHAT WE ARE GIVING OUR ATTENTION TO IS WHAT WE EXPERIENCE MORE OF. WHAT CURRENTLY HAS YOUR ATTENTION?

_____
_____
_____
_____
_____
_____
_____

MY A.M. PRACTICE
FIRST THING WHEN I WAKE UP:

DAY 1
TODAY I FEEL APPRECIATION FOR
_____
_____

THE EMOTIONS I EXPERIENCED UPON AWAKENING WERE
_____ & _____.

_____ 5 - MINUTE VISUALIZATION COMPLETE

Each morning I will awake and immediately think of something to appreciate. Next, I will take about 15 minutes to create my day, MY STORY. I'll design it. I will consciously visualize how my day will play out.

Why do we do this? We all know what it feels like when the alarm doesn't go off and we awake in a panic. For the next 30-60 minutes we have a mini heart attack. We break all morning rituals, we fly out the door, into our day and don't come up for air until we find ourselves "back on schedule."

P.S. You forgot to feed the cat!

P.P.S. If you have kids, multiple the anxiety you felt as you were reading the paragraph above by 100!

Through the practice of creating my own experience I will
- begin to understand the power of my thoughts.
- become selective about which thoughts I choose.
- unlearn patterns of behavior that no longer serve me.

MORNING JOURNAL ENTRIES
- Find something to appreciate
- Identify the dominant emotions
- Complete a short visualization exercise
- Practice a short meditation/creative opportunity
- Incorporate Moving Meditations™.

The thoughts I consciously choose to focus on will eventually turn into new beliefs. My beliefs will steer me in the direction of my desires and re-create my experience. If I want to change my beliefs, I must pay closer attention to my thoughts and HOW THEY MAKE ME FEEL. Only then can I begin choosing different thoughts, create new beliefs and change my experience. This is great news! I have the power to create the life I want through the power of thought.

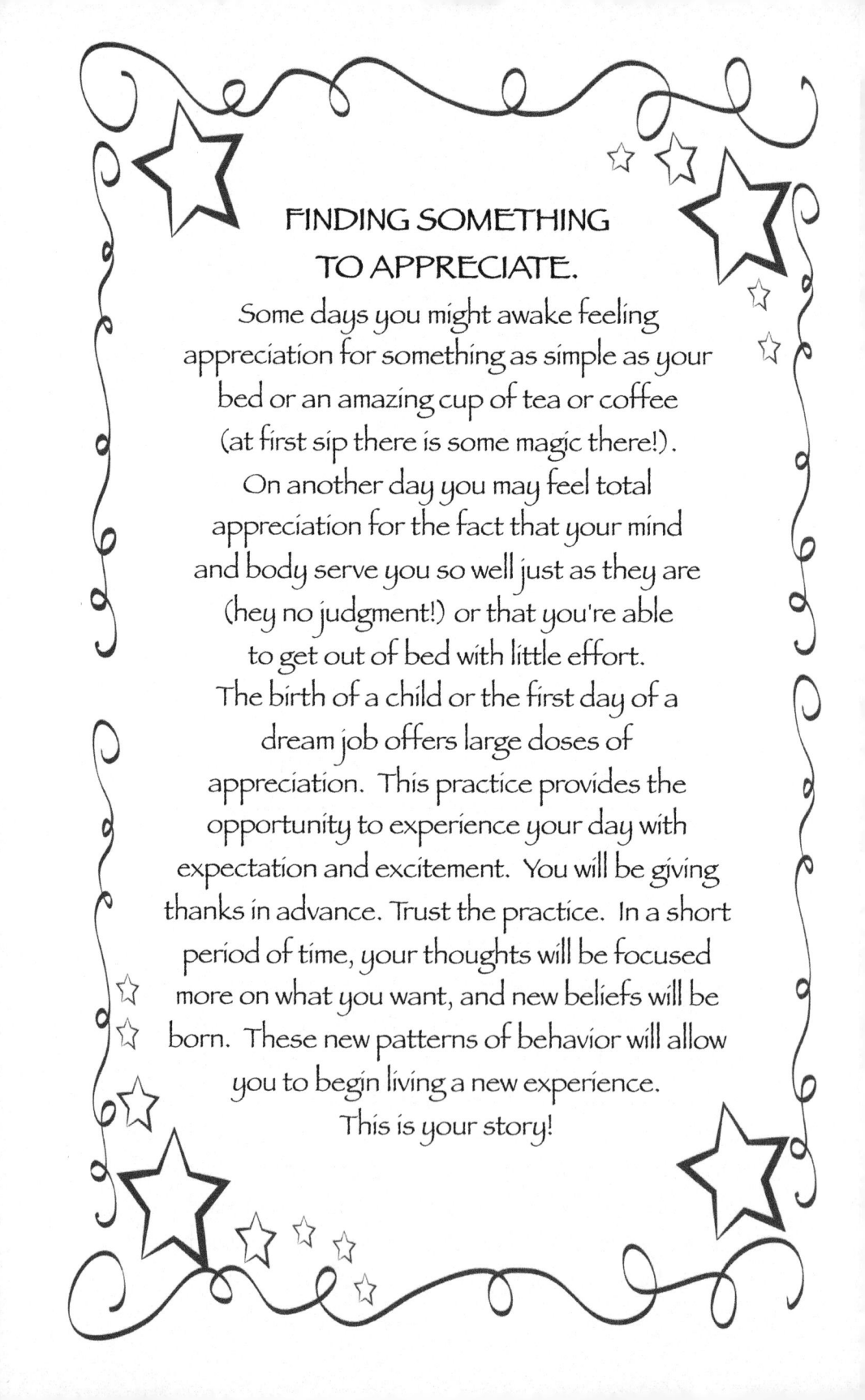

FINDING SOMETHING TO APPRECIATE.

Some days you might awake feeling appreciation for something as simple as your bed or an amazing cup of tea or coffee (at first sip there is some magic there!). On another day you may feel total appreciation for the fact that your mind and body serve you so well just as they are (hey no judgment!) or that you're able to get out of bed with little effort. The birth of a child or the first day of a dream job offers large doses of appreciation. This practice provides the opportunity to experience your day with expectation and excitement. You will be giving thanks in advance. Trust the practice. In a short period of time, your thoughts will be focused more on what you want, and new beliefs will be born. These new patterns of behavior will allow you to begin living a new experience. This is your story!

5-MINUTE VISUALIZATION

Take 5-15 minutes a day to sit with your tea, coffee, or four-legged companion and visualize how you would like your day to unfold. This is a game changer! YOU create your day. YOU choose to visualize your expectation and know that your desires are on their way to you.

EXAMPLE:

I will choose the perfect playlist to chill to on my way to work work today. The music will inspire and relax me. Traffic is typical and no big deal. I'll set the vibe or tone. If I work from home I will do this as I settle into my workspace. Today will be easy. I am remembering that the people I come into contact with are also trying to find their joy. While I may need to interact with them, I will choose who to connect with. This will help me to protect my energy and choose my thoughts carefully. My afternoon meeting is going to be a great learning opportunity. I am confident in my work. I will remember to be quick to listen and slow to speak. I will choose my words carefully before responding. I will remind myself that I have a life and that my job is what I do but does not define who I am. I understand that I can only control how I choose to respond. The rest I release.

Bring it on!

ADDITIONAL EXAMPLES OF VISUALIZATION:

Morning meeting with my least favorite person on the planet who continues to teach me what I don't want to experience in a working relationship.
How will I choose to respond?
NOTE: The Moving Meditation* for DOUBT will help me release any apprehension I have around this subject.
I will use it as needed to help me stay in alignment.
<u>Lunch with mom</u> - Can't wait!
<u>Warrior® Workout</u> - today I will make some time for me, I promise.
<u>Car repair estimate</u> - just a few bucks, I got this!
Examples of emotions possibly connected to these situations:
Morning meeting – Doubt
Lunch – Appreciation
Workout – Love
Car repair – Self-confidence

*see next page

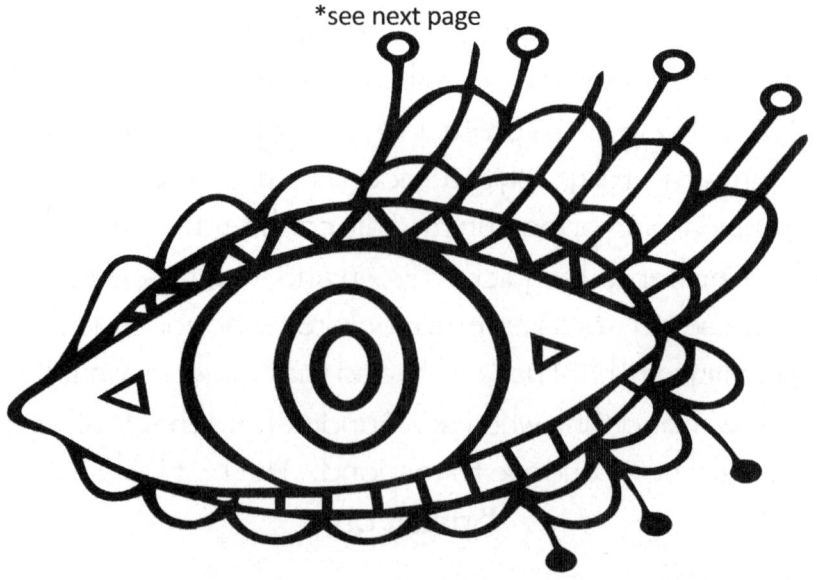

MY P.M. PRACTICE BEFORE GOING TO BED:

Before going to bed at night, I will take about 15 minutes to work the second half of my practice for the day by completing the PM portion of my story page. This will reinforce the belief that I am learning to create my own experience and that I am doing very well. I will remember to be easy about this. Life is supposed to be good for me. Life is supposed to be fun. MY STORY process is no exception.

EVENING JOURNAL ENTRIES
- List the three most dominant emotions I experienced throughout the day.
- How am I feeling about my new practice.
- Additional thoughts around my day and practice.
- Repeat Moving Meditations™ as needed.

GENTLE REMINDER
This is **YOUR STORY**. You can't get this wrong. Pay close attention to how you feel, how you react. Nothing is more important than that **YOU** feel good. This STORYBOOK will help you to identify emotions and begin your practice of shifting with ease. Work the practice. Trust the Universe.

EASY BREEZY

Acknowledging and closing the gaps:

There are always going to be gaps in my life between where I am and where I want to be. By paying attention to how I feel, I can gradually transition and close these gaps. I will begin learning that the gaps are a result of new desires. Once I achieve a desire, new desires are naturally born. My journey lies in the gaps. This is where I will discover or clarify my life's purpose. I will mind the gaps. I will learn that I didn't come here to "get it done" and I can't get this life wrong. I will learn to relax and enjoy this process. When I consistently take 15 minutes to create my day through visualization, I am working the practice and implementing the AE Theory.

AE THEORY:
Paying attention to how we feel ≈
New patterns of behavior

New patterns of behavior ≈
New patterns of thought

New patterns of thought ≈
New beliefs.

New beliefs ≈
A NEW REALITY

What are Moving Meditations™?

Moving Meditations™ are short patterns of movement, connected to an emotion and driven by music, designed to realign or amplify energy.

You will learn to shift energy with ease in order to enhance and improve emotional well-being and experience more joy on a regular basis.

Recognize (and ultimately appreciate) the contrast that exists in life, find clarity around what you want, and begin the process of moving from where you are to where you want to be.

This Moving Meditation Practice will teach you how to

AND LET GO!

MOVING MEDITATIONS™

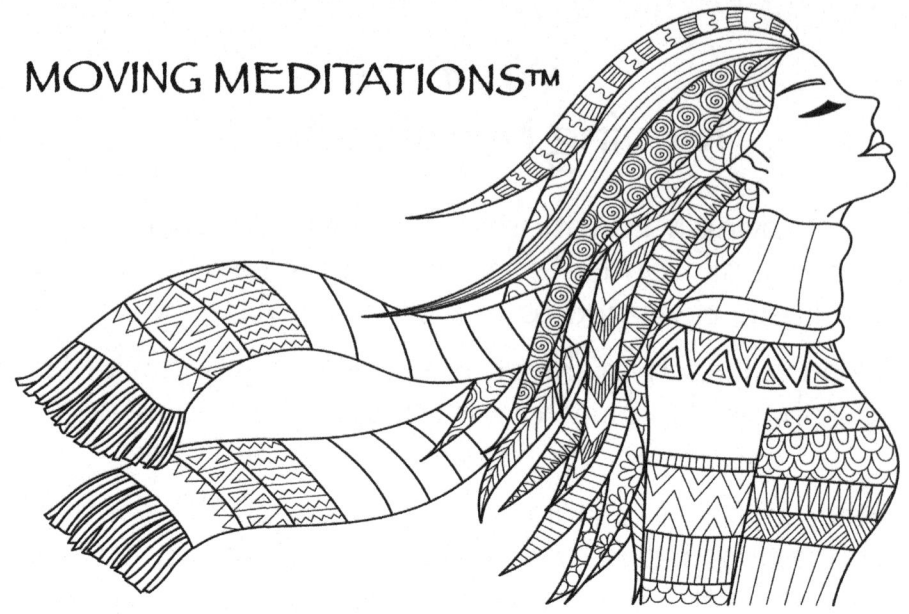

Take time for your Moving Meditations™. Moving Meditations™ will help you to shift from where you are to where you want to be by getting out in front of the emotion before it takes you to a not so good feeling place. Practice them as many times as needed until you begin to feel some relief. If you are doing a MM for JOY, do it even more times! This is the energy we want to live in. While we recognize that we have to know hot to know cold, we understand that everyone wants to mostly live in JOY.
Celebrate in advance!

CELEBRATE!

Selecting Moving Meditations

Selecting the appropriate Moving Meditation™ will become easier as you go deeper into your practice. They will be assigned until you feel comfortable identifying the one that is best suited to help you shift. You may choose one to help you shift or you might choose one that reflects a good feeling. For example, if you are celebrating an achievement (a gap that has been closed) you may choose to do the Moving Meditation™ for joy or celebration. If you are experiencing frustration, you may choose the Moving Meditation™ for frustration or you may feel that you are able to shift quickly and go straight to a relief or self-confidence. Eventually you will find what works best for you.

Remember, no judgment! You are doing well.
Trust the Practice.

The Moving Meditation™ practice is an easy way to begin paying closer attention to how you feel, directing your attention toward what you want and creating new patterns of thought.

Weekly Moving Mediations™ Schedule – Volume I – Course 1

1. Appreciation
2. Compassion
3. Love
4. Frustration
5. Freedom
6. Passion
7. Strength
8. Power
9. Determination
10. Hope
11. Doubt
12. Assurance
13. Recap - Appreciation, Compassion & Love

Volume II – Course 2

1. Reassurance
2. Courage
3. Survival
4. Contrast
5. Resilience
6. Purpose
7. Connection
8. Gratitude
9. Celebration
10. Self-Love
11. Perseverance
12. Forgiveness
13. Recap – Survival, Contrast, Resilience

VOLUME I

LET'S GET STARTED!

Dear Self,

As I begin my journey to living in alignment, I will start by considering the first foundational AE teaching:

Nothing is more important than that I feel good.

This idea feels a bit strange, almost selfish, but I do want to live a happier life so I will commit to giving this idea a chance. After all, I know that I must change my thinking in order to change my experience. I can honestly say that how I feel does matter. In the past, I haven't always put my own feelings first. I am eager to change this behavior.

I look forward to a quieter mind as I am often exhausted by own thoughts and the way they make me feel.

I am a bit nervous about exposing myself to a new tribe, but I am also excited to have an entirely new group of like-minded people who support me and are seeking a similar experience.

I will be brave and allow myself to have fun along the way.

I deserve to be happy,

Me

VOLUME I

NOTHING IS MORE IMPORTANT THAN THAT I FEEL GOOD!

IT'S TIME TO GROW.

DAY 1 DATE _____

TODAY I FEEL APPRECIATION FOR

_____

_____

THE EMOTIONS I EXPERIENCED UPON AWAKENING WERE

_____

& _____.

__ 5 - MINUTE VISUALIZATION COMPLETE

__ MOVING MEDITATION FOR APPRECIATION

The three most dominant emotions
I experienced today were:

Fear	Trust	Anticipation
Surprise	Anger	Appreciation
Jealousy	Loneliness	_____
Happiness	Sadness	_____

(a gentle reminder to refer to word list at the back of your journal)

I feel as though:

A) I am more/less relaxed about everything in general

B) I'm _____ to have a practice and process to follow for my journey

C) I'm _____ that this will work for me.

   1) Doubting   2) Hopeful   3) Confident

Additional thoughts:
_____
_____
_____
_____
_____
_____
_____

YOU JUST HAVE TO GET STARTED!

DAY 2   DATE _____

TODAY I FEEL APPRECIATION FOR
_____
_____

THE EMOTIONS I EXPERIENCED UPON AWAKENING WERE
_____
& _____.

__ 5 - MINUTE VISUALIZATION COMPLETE
__ MOVING MEDITATION FOR APPRECIATION

SOMETIMES IT'S EASIER TO QUIET MY MIND WHEN I'M MOVING.

The three most dominant emotions
I experienced today were:

Fear	Trust	Anticipation
Surprise	Anger	Appreciation
Jealousy	Loneliness	_____
Happiness	Sadness	_____

I feel as though:
A) I am more/less relaxed about everything in general
B) I'm _____ to have a practice and process to follow for my journey
C) I'm _____ that this will work for me.
    1) Doubting   2) Hopeful   3) Confident

Additional thoughts:
_____
_____
_____
_____
_____
_____
_____

THIS LIFE IS MY RIDE, I DECIDE

DAY 3   DATE _____

TODAY I FEEL APPRECIATION FOR
_____
_____

THE EMOTIONS I EXPERIENCED UPON AWAKENING WERE
_____
& _____.

__ 5 - MINUTE VISUALIZATION COMPLETE
__ MOVING MEDITATION FOR APPRECIATION

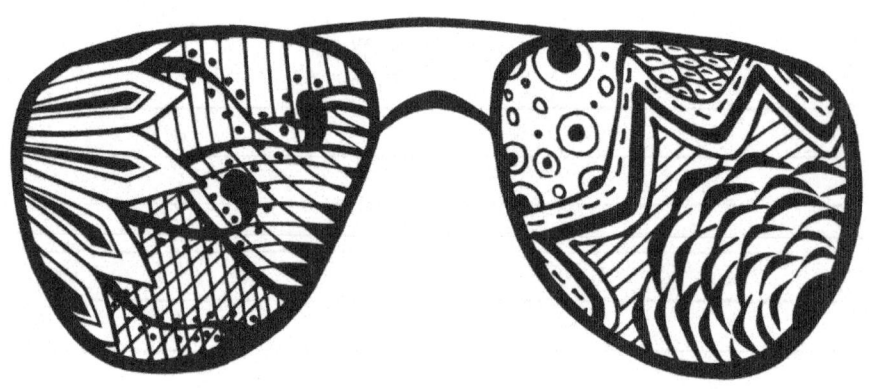

I'M BEGINNING TO SEE THINGS DIFFERENTLY.

The three most dominant emotions I experienced today were:

Fear	Trust	Anticipation
Surprise	Anger	Appreciation
Jealousy	Loneliness	_____
Happiness	Sadness	_____

I feel as though:

A) I am more/less relaxed about everything in general

B) I'm _____ to have a practice and process to follow for my journey

C) I'm _____ that this will work for me.

1)   1) Doubting   2) Hopeful   3) Confident

Additional thoughts:
_____
_____
_____
_____
_____
_____
_____

JUST DO YOU!

DAY 4   DATE _____

TODAY I FEEL APPRECIATION FOR
_____
_____

THE EMOTIONS I EXPERIENCED UPON AWAKENING WERE
_____
& _____.

__ 5 - MINUTE VISUALIZATION COMPLETE
__ MOVING MEDITATION FOR APPRECIATION

I AM LEARNING TO SIT QUIETLY.

The three most dominant emotions I experienced today were:

Fear	Trust	Anticipation
Surprise	Anger	Appreciation
Jealousy	Loneliness	_____
Happiness	Sadness	_____

I feel as though:

A) I am more/less relaxed about everything in general

B) I'm _____ to have a practice and process to follow for my journey

C) I'm _____ that this will work for me.

   1) Doubting   2) Hopeful   3) Confident

Additional thoughts:

_____
_____
_____
_____
_____
_____
_____

THE ONLY THING WE CAN TRULY CONTROL IS OUR THOUGHTS.

DAY 5   DATE _____

TODAY I FEEL APPRECIATION FOR
_____
_____

THE EMOTIONS I EXPERIENCED UPON AWAKENING WERE
_____
& _____.

__ 5 - MINUTE VISUALIZATION COMPLETE
__ MOVING MEDITATION FOR APPRECIATION

IT'S NOT ALWAYS EASY TO PUT THOUGHTS TO PAPER.

The three most dominant emotions
I experienced today were:

Fear	Trust	Anticipation
Surprise	Anger	Appreciation
Jealousy	Loneliness	_____
Happiness	Sadness	_____

I feel as though:
A) I am more/less relaxed about everything in general
B) I'm _____ to have a practice and process to follow for my journey
C) I'm _____ that this will work for me.
  1) Doubting   2) Hopeful   3) Confident

Additional thoughts:
_____
_____
_____
_____
_____
_____
_____

TODAY I BEGIN WRITING MY STORY. ONE NEW THOUGHT AT A TIME.

DAY 6   DATE _____

TODAY I FEEL APPRECIATION FOR
_____
_____

THE EMOTIONS I EXPERIENCED UPON AWAKENING WERE
_____
& _____.

__ 5 - MINUTE VISUALIZATION COMPLETE
__ MOVING MEDITATION FOR APPRECIATION

AM I RUNNING OUT OF TIME?

The three most dominant emotions
I experienced today were:

Fear	Trust	Anticipation
Surprise	Anger	Appreciation
Jealousy	Loneliness	_____
Happiness	Sadness	_____

I feel as though:

A) I am more/less relaxed about everything in general

B) I'm _____ to have a practice and process to follow for my journey

C) I'm _____ that this will work for me.

    1) Doubting   2) Hopeful   3) Confident

Additional thoughts:
_____
_____
_____
_____
_____
_____
_____

NOW
LIVE IN IT!

DAY 7   DATE _____

TODAY I FEEL APPRECIATION FOR
_____
_____

THE EMOTIONS I EXPERIENCED UPON AWAKENING WERE
_____
& _____.

__ 5 - MINUTE VISUALIZATION COMPLETE
__ MOVING MEDITATION FOR APPRECIATION

I AM BEGINNING TO FEEL MORE BALANCED.

The three most dominant emotions
I experienced today were:

Fear	Trust	Anticipation
Surprise	Anger	Appreciation
Jealousy	Loneliness	_____
Happiness	Sadness	_____

I feel as though:

A) I am more/less relaxed about everything in general

B) I'm _____ to have a practice and process to follow for my journey

C) I'm _____ that this will work for me.

    1) Doubting   2) Hopeful   3) Confident

Additional thoughts:

_____
_____
_____
_____
_____
_____
_____

STAYING IN ALIGNMENT IS ESSENTIAL TO MY WELL-BEING.

DAY 8   DATE _____

TODAY I FEEL APPRECIATION FOR
_____
_____

THE EMOTIONS I EXPERIENCED UPON AWAKENING WERE
_____
& _____.

__ 5 - MINUTE VISUALIZATION COMPLETE
__ MOVING MEDITATION FOR APPRECIATION
__ MOVING MEDITATION FOR COMPASSION

DREAMING IS WHAT I DO!

The three most dominant emotions
I experienced today were:

Fear	Trust	Anticipation
Surprise	Anger	Appreciation
Jealousy	Loneliness	_____
Happiness	Sadness	_____

I feel as though:

A) I am more/less relaxed about everything in general

B) I'm _____ to have a practice and process to follow for my journey

C) I'm _____ that this will work for me.

    1) Doubting   2) Hopeful   3) Confident

Additional thoughts:

_____
_____
_____
_____
_____
_____
_____

LIFE IS SUPPOSED TO BE GOOD FOR ME.

DAY 9   DATE _____

TODAY I FEEL APPRECIATION FOR
_____
_____

THE EMOTIONS I EXPERIENCED UPON AWAKENING WERE
_____
& _____.

__ 5 - MINUTE VISUALIZATION COMPLETE
__ MOVING MEDITATION FOR APPRECIATION
__ MOVING MEDITATION FOR COMPASSION

THINGS ARE ALWAYS MOVING!

The three most dominant emotions I experienced today were:

Fear   Trust   Anticipation
Surprise   Anger   Appreciation
Jealousy   Loneliness   _____
Happiness   Sadness   _____

I feel as though:

A) I am more/less relaxed about everything in general
B) I'm _____ to have a practice and process to follow for my journey
C) I'm _____ that this will work for me.

    1) Doubting   2) Hopeful   3) Confident

Additional thoughts:

_____
_____
_____
_____
_____
_____
_____
_____

CHANGE IS ALWAYS COMING.

DAY 10   DATE _____

TODAY I FEEL APPRECIATION FOR
_____
_____

THE EMOTIONS I EXPERIENCED UPON AWAKENING WERE
_____
& _____.

__ 5-MINUTE VISUALIZATION COMPLETE
__ MOVING MEDITATION FOR APPRECIATION
__ MOVING MEDITATION FOR COMPASSION

I ALWAYS BLOCK OFF ME TIME!

The three most dominant emotions
I experienced today were:

Fear	Trust	Anticipation
Surprise	Anger	Appreciation
Jealousy	Loneliness	_____
Happiness	Sadness	_____

I feel as though:
A) I am more/less relaxed about everything in general
B) I'm _____ to have a practice and process to follow for my journey
C) I'm _____ that this will work for me.
   1) Doubting   2) Hopeful   3) Confident

Additional thoughts:
_____
_____
_____
_____
_____
_____
_____

I AM MY BIGGEST PRIORITY.

DAY 11   DATE _____

TODAY I FEEL APPRECIATION FOR
_____
_____

THE EMOTIONS I EXPERIENCED UPON AWAKENING WERE
_____
& _____.

__ 5 - MINUTE VISUALIZATION COMPLETE
__ MOVING MEDITATION FOR APPRECIATION
__ MOVING MEDITATION FOR COMPASSION

BEAUTIFUL SURPRISES ARE ALL AROUND ME!

The three most dominant emotions
I experienced today were:

Fear	Trust	Anticipation
Surprise	Anger	Appreciation
Jealousy	Loneliness	_____
Happiness	Sadness	_____

I feel as though:

A) I am more/less relaxed about everything in general

B) I'm _____ to have a practice and process to follow for my journey

C) I'm _____ that this will work for me.

    1) Doubting   2) Hopeful   3) Confident

Additional thoughts:

_____
_____
_____
_____
_____
_____
_____

I KEEP AN OPEN MIND AND THINK OUTSIDE THE BOX.

DAY 12   DATE _____

TODAY I FEEL APPRECIATION FOR
_____
_____

THE EMOTIONS I EXPERIENCED UPON AWAKENING WERE
_____
& _____.

__ 5 - MINUTE VISUALIZATION COMPLETE
__ MOVING MEDITATION FOR APPRECIATION
__ MOVING MEDITATION FOR COMPASSION

MANY ACTIVITIES HELP ME TO QUIET MY MIND!

The three most dominant emotions I experienced today were:

Fear	Trust	Anticipation
Surprise	Anger	Appreciation
Jealousy	Loneliness	_____
Happiness	Sadness	_____

I feel as though:

A) I am more/less relaxed about everything in general

B) I'm _____ to have a practice and process to follow for my journey

C) I'm _____ that this will work for me.

    1) Doubting   2) Hopeful   3) Confident

Additional thoughts:

_____
_____
_____
_____
_____
_____
_____

QUIET YOUR MIND, EMPOWER YOUR BODY.

DAY 13   DATE _____

TODAY I FEEL APPRECIATION FOR
_____
_____

THE EMOTIONS I EXPERIENCED UPON AWAKENING WERE
_____
& _____.

__ 5 - MINUTE VISUALIZATION COMPLETE
__ MOVING MEDITATION FOR APPRECIATION
__ MOVING MEDITATION FOR COMPASSION

I AM COURAGEOUS!

The three most dominant emotions I experienced today were:

Fear	Trust	Anticipation
Surprise	Anger	Appreciation
Jealousy	Loneliness	_____
Happiness	Sadness	_____

I feel as though:

A) I am more/less relaxed about everything in general

B) I'm _____ to have a practice and process to follow for my journey

C) I'm _____ that this will work for me.

   1) Doubting   2) Hopeful   3) Confident

Additional thoughts:
_____
_____
_____
_____
_____
_____
_____

I AM STRONG.

DAY 14   DATE _____

TODAY I FEEL APPRECIATION FOR
_____
_____

THE EMOTIONS I EXPERIENCED UPON AWAKENING WERE
_____
& _____.

__ 5 - MINUTE VISUALIZATION COMPLETE
__ MOVING MEDITATION FOR APPRECIATION
__ MOVING MEDITATION FOR COMPASSION

WHEN I LISTEN, EVERYTHING SPEAKS TO ME!

The three most dominant emotions
I experienced today were:

Fear	Trust	Anticipation
Surprise	Anger	Appreciation
Jealousy	Loneliness	_____
Happiness	Sadness	_____

I feel as though:
A) I am more/less relaxed about everything in general
B) I'm _____ to have a practice and process to follow for my journey
C) I'm _____ that this will work for me.

    1) Doubting   2) Hopeful   3) Confident

Additional thoughts:
_____
_____
_____
_____
_____
_____
_____

THE BEST COMPANY I KEEP IS MY OWN.

DAY 15   DATE _____

TODAY I FEEL APPRECIATION FOR
_____
_____

THE EMOTIONS I EXPERIENCED UPON AWAKENING WERE
_____
& _____.

__ 5 - MINUTE VISUALIZATION COMPLETE
__ MOVING MEDITATION FOR APPRECIATION
__ MOVING MEDITATION FOR LOVE

I LIVE IN HARMONY WITH ALL CREATURES!

The three most dominant emotions I experienced today were:

Fear	Trust	Anticipation
Surprise	Anger	Appreciation
Jealousy	Loneliness	_____
Happiness	Sadness	_____

I feel as though:

A) I am more/less relaxed about everything in general

B) I'm _____ to have a practice and process to follow for my journey

C) I'm _____ that this will work for me.

    1) Doubting   2) Hopeful   3) Confident

Additional thoughts:

_____
_____
_____
_____
_____
_____
_____
_____

MOTHER EARTH IS HOME TO MANY.

DAY 16   DATE _____

TODAY I FEEL APPRECIATION FOR
_____
_____

THE EMOTIONS I EXPERIENCED UPON AWAKENING WERE
_____
& _____.

__ 5 - MINUTE VISUALIZATION COMPLETE
__ MOVING MEDITATION FOR APPRECIATION
__ MOVING MEDITATION FOR LOVE

IT'S PLAYTIME!

The three most dominant emotions
I experienced today were:

Dissatisfied	Amazed	Irritated
Reassured	Compassionate	Ashamed
Kind	Ecstatic	Thankful

_____

I feel as though:

I am _____

_____

_____.

I am using this practice to _____

_____

_____.

I am _____ this practice is working for me.

Additional thoughts:

_____
_____
_____
_____
_____
_____
_____
_____

I'M JUST A BIG KID!

DAY 17   DATE _____

TODAY I FEEL APPRECIATION FOR
_____
_____

THE EMOTIONS I EXPERIENCED UPON AWAKENING WERE
_____
& _____.

__ 5 - MINUTE VISUALIZATION COMPLETE
__ MOVING MEDITATION FOR APPRECIATION
__ MOVING MEDITATION FOR LOVE

THE UNIVERSE IS MY PLAYGROUND!

The three most dominant emotions I experienced today were:

Dissatisfied	Amazed	Irritated
Reassured	Compassionate	Ashamed
Kind	Ecstatic	Thankful

_____

I feel as though:

I am _____
_____
_____.

I am using this practice to _____
_____
_____.

I am _____ this practice is working for me.

Additional thoughts:
_____
_____
_____
_____
_____
_____
_____
_____
_____

I AM A WORLD CHANGER

DAY 18   DATE _____

TODAY I FEEL APPRECIATION FOR
_____
_____

THE EMOTIONS I EXPERIENCED UPON AWAKENING WERE
_____
& _____.

__ 5 - MINUTE VISUALIZATION COMPLETE
__ MOVING MEDITATION FOR APPRECIATION
__ MOVING MEDITATION FOR LOVE

AS A WARRIOR, I HAVE A DEEPER UNDERSTANDING OF WHO I AM.

The three most dominant emotions I experienced today were:

Dissatisfied	Amazed	Irritated
Reassured	Compassionate	Ashamed
Kind	Ecstatic	Thankful

_____

I feel as though:

I am _____
_____
_____.

I am using this practice to _____
_____
_____.

I am _____ this practice is working for me.

Additional thoughts:
_____
_____
_____
_____
_____
_____
_____
_____

GRATEFUL WARRIOR

DAY 19   DATE _____

TODAY I FEEL APPRECIATION FOR
_____
_____

THE EMOTIONS I EXPERIENCED UPON AWAKENING WERE
_____
& _____.

__ 5 - MINUTE VISUALIZATION COMPLETE
__ MOVING MEDITATION FOR APPRECIATION
__ MOVING MEDITATION FOR LOVE

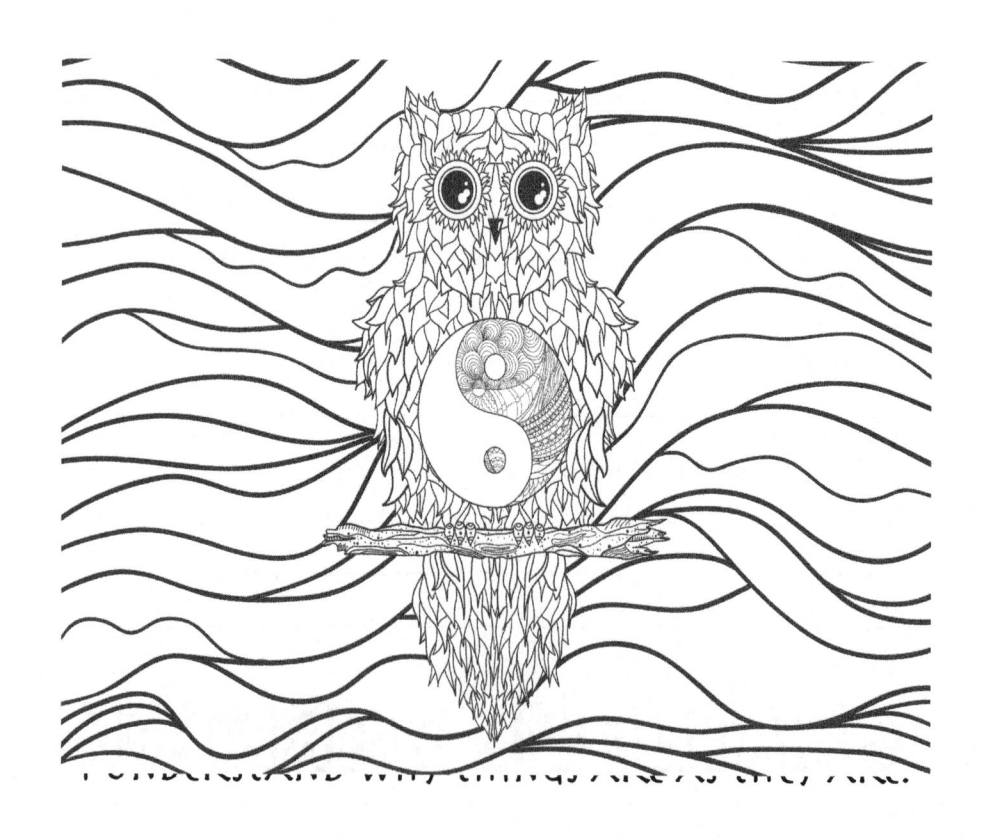

The three most dominant emotions
I experienced today were:

Dissatisfied	Amazed	Irritated
Reassured	Compassionate	Ashamed
Kind	Ecstatic	Thankful

_____

I feel as though:

I am _____
_____
_____,

I am using this practice to _____
_____
_____,

I am _____ this practice is working for me.

Additional thoughts:
_____
_____
_____
_____
_____
_____
_____
_____
_____
_____

I AM WISE.

DAY 20   DATE _____

TODAY I FEEL APPRECIATION FOR
_____
_____

THE EMOTIONS I EXPERIENCED UPON AWAKENING WERE
_____
& _____.

__ 5-MINUTE VISUALIZATION COMPLETE
__ MOVING MEDITATION FOR APPRECIATION
__ MOVING MEDITATION FOR LOVE

WHAT AM I GIVING MY ATTENTION TO?

The three most dominant emotions
I experienced today were:

Dissatisfied	Amazed	Irritated
Reassured	Compassionate	Ashamed
Kind	Ecstatic	Thankful

_____

I feel as though:

I am _____
_____
_____.

I am using this practice to _____
_____
_____.

I am _____ this practice is working for me.

Additional thoughts:
_____
_____
_____
_____
_____
_____
_____

WHAT I THINK ABOUT BECOMES MY REALITY.

DAY 21   DATE _____

TODAY I FEEL APPRECIATION FOR
_____
_____

THE EMOTIONS I EXPERIENCED UPON AWAKENING WERE
_____
& _____.

__ 5 - MINUTE VISUALIZATION COMPLETE
__ MOVING MEDITATION FOR APPRECIATION
__ MOVING MEDITATION FOR LOVE

I LOVE RECEIVING COMPLIMENTS.

The three most dominant emotions
I experienced today were:

Dissatisfied	Amazed	Irritated
Reassured	Compassionate	Ashamed
Kind	Ecstatic	Thankful

_____

I feel as though:

I am _____
_____
_____.

I am using this practice to _____
_____
_____.

I am _____ this practice is working for me.

Additional thoughts:
_____
_____
_____
_____
_____
_____
_____
_____
_____
_____
_____
_____

I AM ENOUGH.

DAY 22   DATE _____

TODAY I FEEL APPRECIATION FOR
_____
_____

THE EMOTIONS I EXPERIENCED UPON AWAKENING WERE
_____
& _____.

__ 5 - MINUTE VISUALIZATION COMPLETE
__ MOVING MEDITATIONS

WHAT'S IN BETWEEN MATTERS!

The three most dominant emotions
I experienced today were:

Dissatisfied	Amazed	Irritated
Reassured	Compassionate	Ashamed
Kind	Ecstatic	Thankful

_____

I feel as though:

I am _____
_____
_____.

I am using this practice to _____
_____
_____.

I am _____ this practice is working for me.

Additional thoughts:
_____
_____
_____
_____
_____
_____
_____
_____

THE BEST PART OF LIFE HAPPENS IN THE GAPS.

DAY 23   DATE _____

TODAY I FEEL APPRECIATION FOR
_____
_____

THE EMOTIONS I EXPERIENCED UPON AWAKENING WERE
_____
& _____.

__ 5 - MINUTE VISUALIZATION COMPLETE
__ MOVING MEDITATIONS

I HAVE A CONNECTION TO FAR AWAY PLACES!

The three most dominant emotions
I experienced today were:

Dissatisfied	Amazed	Irritated
Reassured	Compassionate	Ashamed
Kind	Ecstatic	Thankful

_____

I feel as though:

I am _____
_____
_____.

I am using this practice to _____
_____
_____.

I am _____ this practice is working for me.

Additional thoughts:
_____
_____
_____
_____
_____
_____
_____
_____
_____
_____
_____
_____

I LOVE USING MY IMAGINATION.

DAY 24   DATE _____

TODY I FEEL APPRECIATION FOR
_____
_____

THE EMOTIONS I EXPERIENCED UPON AWAKENING WERE
_____
& _____.

__ 5 - MINUTE VISUALIZATION COMPLETE
__ MOVING MEDITATIONS

I NAP FREQUENTLY AND WITHOUT GUILT.

The three most dominant emotions
I experienced today were:

Dissatisfied	Amazed	Irritated
Reassured	Compassionate	Ashamed
Kind	Ecstatic	Thankful

_____

I feel as though:

I am _____
_____
_____.

I am using this practice to _____
_____
_____.

I am _____ this practice is working for me.

Additional thoughts:
_____
_____
_____
_____
_____
_____
_____
_____
_____
_____
_____
_____

WHEN I NEED TO SLOW MOMENTUM, I TAKE A NAP.

DAY 25　　　DATE _____

TODAY I FEEL APPRECIATION FOR
_____
_____

THE EMOTIONS I EXPERIENCED UPON AWAKENING WERE
_____
& _____.

__ 5 - MINUTE VISUALIZATION COMPLETE
__ MOVING MEDITATIONS

I ALWAYS MAKE TIME FOR MUSIC!

The three most dominant emotions
I experienced today were:

Dissatisfied	Amazed	Irritated
Reassured	Compassionate	Ashamed
Kind	Ecstatic	Thankful

_____

I feel as though:

I am _____
_____
_____.

I am using this practice to _____
_____
_____.

I am _____ this practice is working for me.

Additional thoughts:
_____
_____
_____
_____
_____
_____
_____
_____
_____
_____
_____
_____
_____
_____

MUSIC EMPOWERS ME.

DAY 26   DATE _____

TODAY I FEEL APPRECIATION FOR
_____
_____

THE EMOTIONS I EXPERIENCED UPON AWAKENING WERE
_____
& _____.

_ 5 - MINUTE VISUALIZATION COMPLETE
_ MOVING MEDITATIONS

SOMETIMES CHANGING OUR VIEW CHANGES OUR PERSPECTIVE.

The three most dominant emotions I experienced today were:

Dissatisfied	Amazed	Irritated
Reassured	Compassionate	Ashamed
Kind	Ecstatic	Thankful

_____

I feel as though:

I am _____
_____
_____.

I am using this practice to _____
_____
_____.

I am _____ this practice is working for me.

Additional thoughts:
_____
_____
_____
_____
_____
_____
_____
_____

I WILL RECONSIDER MY PERSPECTIVE.

DAY 27   DATE _____

TODAY I FEEL APPRECIATION FOR
_____
_____

THE EMOTIONS I EXPERIENCED UPON AWAKENING WERE
_____
& _____.

__ 5 - MINUTE VISUALIZATION COMPLETE
__ MOVING MEDITATIONS

DON'T FORGET TO LOOK UP!

The three most dominant emotions
I experienced today were:

Dissatisfied	Amazed	Irritated
Reassured	Compassionate	Ashamed
Kind	Ecstatic	Thankful

_____

I feel as though:

I am _____
_____
_____.

I am using this practice to _____
_____
_____.

I am _____ this practice is working for me.

Additional thoughts:
_____
_____
_____
_____
_____
_____
_____
_____
_____
_____
_____
_____

THE TRUTH SHINES.

DAY 28   DATE _____

TODAY I FEEL APPRECIATION FOR
_____
_____

THE EMOTIONS I EXPERIENCED UPON AWAKENING WERE
_____
& _____.

__ 5 - MINUTE VISUALIZATION COMPLETE
__ MOVING MEDITATIONS

I TAP INTO MY POWER.

The three most dominant emotions
I experienced today were:

Dissatisfied	Amazed	Irritated
Reassured	Compassionate	Ashamed
Kind	Ecstatic	Thankful

_____

I feel as though:

I am _____
_____
_____.

I am using this practice to _____
_____
_____.

I am _____ this practice is working for me.

Additional thoughts:
_____
_____
_____
_____
_____
_____
_____
_____
_____

THE PRACTICE OF BALANCE IS ONGOING.

DAY 29   DATE _____

TODAY I FEEL APPRECIATION FOR
_____
_____

THE EMOTIONS I EXPERIENCED UPON
AWAKENING WERE
_____
& _____.

__ 5 - MINUTE VISUALIZATION COMPLETE
__ MOVING MEDITATIONS

I HAVE A WARRIOR STATE OF MIND.

The three most dominant emotions
I experienced today were:

Dissatisfied	Amazed	Irritated
Reassured	Compassionate	Ashamed
Kind	Ecstatic	Thankful

_____

I feel as though:

I am _____
_____
_____.

I am using this practice to _____
_____
_____.

I am _____ this practice is working for me.

Additional thoughts:
_____
_____
_____
_____
_____
_____
_____
_____
_____

THIS WORK IS MY FOOD.

DAY 30   DATE _____

TODAY I FEEL APPRECIATION FOR
_____
_____

THE EMOTIONS I EXPERIENCED UPON AWAKENING WERE
_____
& _____.

__ 5-MINUTE VISUALIZATION COMPLETE
__ MOVING MEDITATIONS

I AM CREATING A HOME WHERE I EXPERIENCE PEACE OF MIND, SAFETY, LOVE & COMPASSION.

The three most dominant emotions I experienced today were:

Dissatisfied   Amazed   Irritated
Reassured   Compassionate   Ashamed
Kind   Ecstatic   Thankful

_____

I feel as though:

I am _____
_____
_____.

I am using this practice to _____
_____
_____.

I am _____ this practice is working for me.

Additional thoughts:

_____
_____
_____
_____
_____
_____
_____
_____
_____

I ALWAYS FIND MY WAY HOME.

DAY 31   DATE _____

I APPRECIATE
_____

The emotions I experienced upon awakening were
_____ & _____

Moving Meditations completed
_____
_____

Subjects that came to mind during visualization practice
_____
_____
_____

The three most dominant emotions/ feelings I experienced today were:

Calm	Peaceful	Passionate
Intrigued	Concerned	Comforted
Uneasy	Paralyzed	Desperate

_____   _____   _____

I feel as though
I am more _____ about my life.
Relaxed   Excited   Confident
I am _____ with this practice.
Comfortable   Frustrated   Happier

Paying attention to how I feel has helped me to
_____
_____
_____
_____

Be more selfish
Find more balance
Be more patient with others

EVERYTHING IS GOING TO BE OK.

DAY 32   DATE_____

I APPRECIATE

_____

The emotions I experienced upon awakening were

_____ & _____

Moving Meditations completed

_____

_____

Subjects that came to mind during visualization practice

_____
_____
_____
_____
_____
_____
_____

The three most dominant emotions/
feelings I experienced today were:

Calm	Peaceful	Passionate
Intrigued	Concerned	Comforted
Uneasy	Paralyzed	Desperate

_____   _____   _____

I feel as though
I am more _____ about my life.
Relaxed   Excited   Confident
I am _____ with this practice.
Comfortable   Frustrated   Happier

Paying attention to how I feel has helped me to

_____
_____
_____
_____

Be more selfish
Find more balance
Be more patient with others

BUILD YOUR OWN WORLD.

DAY 33   DATE_____

I APPRECIATE
_____

The emotions I experienced upon awakening were
_____&_____

Moving Meditations completed
_____
_____

Subjects that came to mind during visualization practice
_____
_____
_____
_____
_____
_____

The three most dominant emotions/ feelings I experienced today were:

Calm	Peaceful	Passionate
Intrigued	Concerned	Comforted
Uneasy	Paralyzed	Desperate

_____ _____ _____

I feel as though
I am more _____ about my life.
Relaxed   Excited   Confident

I am _____ with this practice.
Comfortable   Frustrated   Happier

Paying attention to how I feel has helped me to
_____
_____
_____
_____

Be more selfish
Find more balance
Be more patient with others

YA GOTTA GROW!

DAY 34   DATE_____

I APPRECIATE
_____

The emotions I experienced upon awakening were
_____ & _____

Moving Meditations completed
_____
_____

Subjects that came to mind during visualization practice
_____
_____
_____
_____

The three most dominant emotions/ feelings I experienced today were:

Calm	Peaceful	Passionate
Intrigued	Concerned	Comforted
Uneasy	Paralyzed	Desperate
_____	_____	_____

I feel as though
I am more _____ about my life.
Relaxed　　　　　Excited　　　　　Confident
I am _____ with this practice.
Comfortable　　　Frustrated　　　Happier

Paying attention to how I feel has helped me to

_____
_____
_____
_____
_____

Be more selfish
Find more balance
Be more patient with others

MINDSHIFT.

DAY 35   DATE_____

I APPRECIATE
_____

The emotions I experienced upon awakening were
_____ & _____

Moving Meditations completed
_____
_____

Subjects that came to mind during visualization practice
_____
_____
_____
_____

The three most dominant emotions/
feelings I experienced today were:

Calm	Peaceful	Passionate
Intrigued	Concerned	Comforted
Uneasy	Paralyzed	Desperate

_____ _____ _____

I feel as though
I am more _____ about my life.

Relaxed   Excited   Confident

I am _____ with this practice.

Comfortable   Frustrated   Happier

Paying attention to how I feel has helped me to

_____
_____
_____
_____
_____
_____

Be more selfish
Find more balance
Be more patient with others

FREE HUGS!

DAY 36   DATE_____

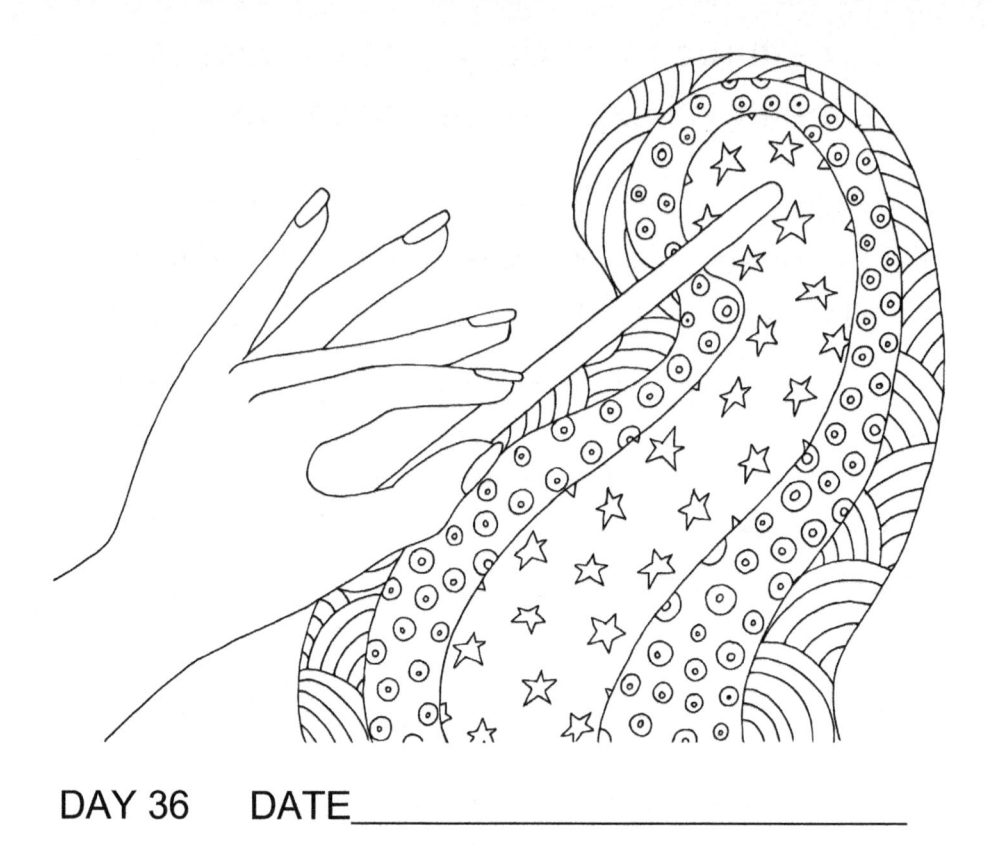

I APPRECIATE
_____
The emotions I experienced upon awakening were
_____&_____
Moving Meditations completed
_____
_____
Subjects that came to mind during visualization practice
_____
_____
_____
_____
_____
_____
_____

The three most dominant emotions/
feelings I experienced today were:

Calm	Peaceful	Passionate
Intrigued	Concerned	Comforted
Uneasy	Paralyzed	Desperate

_____ _____ _____

I feel as though
I am more _____ about my life.
Relaxed   Excited   Confident
I am _____ with this practice.
Comfortable   Frustrated   Happier

Paying attention to how I feel has helped me to

_____
_____
_____
_____
_____
_____

Be more selfish
Find more balance
Be more patient with others

THE POWER OF THOUGHT IS MAGICAL.

DAY 37   DATE_____

I APPRECIATE

_____

The emotions I experienced upon awakening were
_____ & _____

Moving Meditations completed

_____

_____

Subjects that came to mind during visualization practice

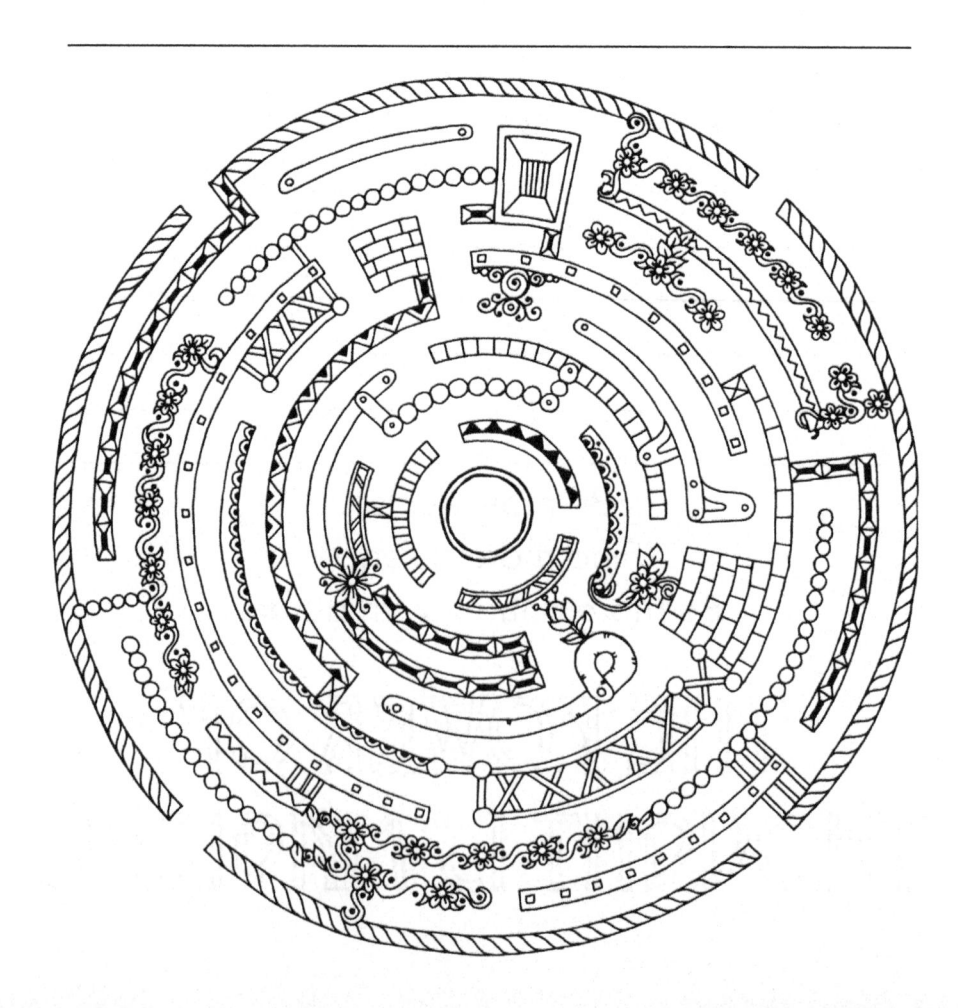

_____

_____

_____

The three most dominant emotions/
feelings I experienced today were:

Calm	Peaceful	Passionate
Intrigued	Concerned	Comforted
Uneasy	Paralyzed	Desperate

_____   _____   _____

I feel as though
I am more _____ about my life.
Relaxed   Excited   Confident

I am _____ with this practice.
Comfortable   Frustrated   Happier

Paying attention to how I feel has helped me to
_____
_____
_____
_____
_____

Be more selfish
Find more balance
Be more patient with others

I CHOOSE THE PATH OF LEAST RESISTANCE.

DAY 38   DATE_____

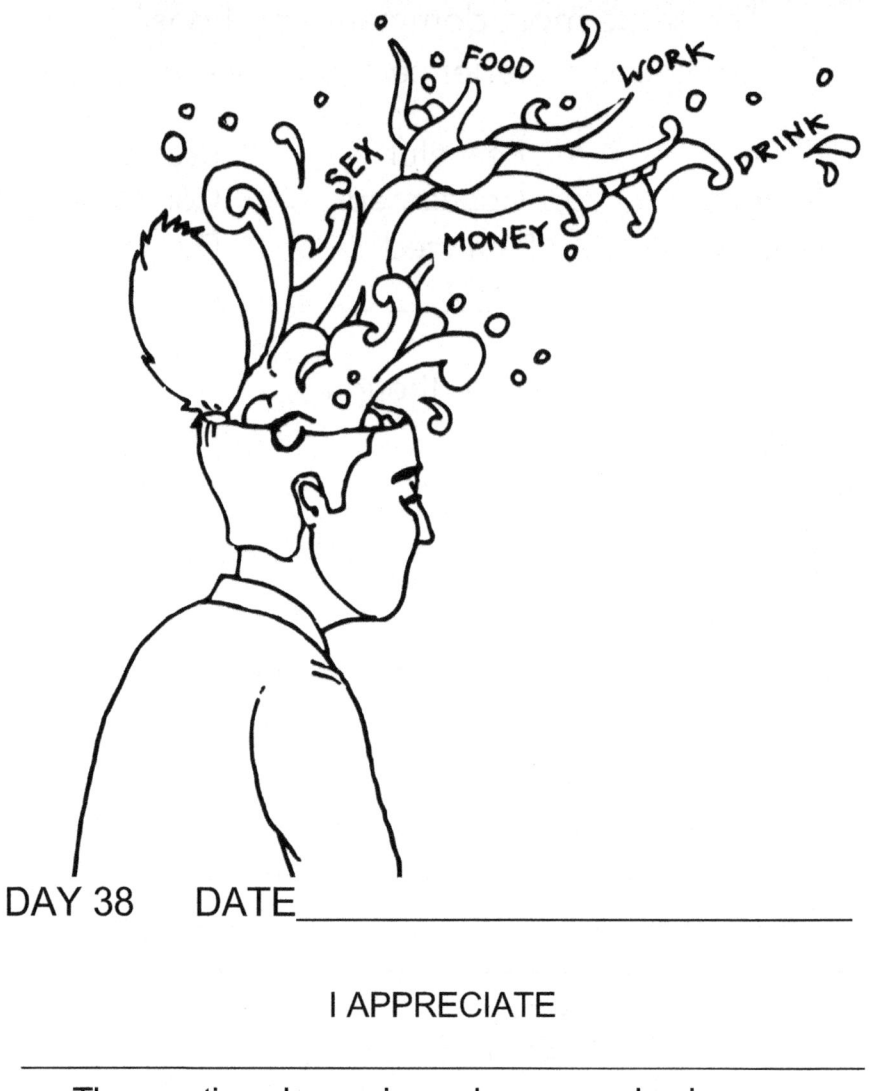

I APPRECIATE
_____
The emotions I experienced upon awakening were
_____ & _____
Moving Meditations completed
_____
_____

Subjects that came to mind during visualization practice
_____
_____
_____
_____
_____

The three most dominant emotions/
feelings I experienced today were:

Calm	Peaceful	Passionate
Intrigued	Concerned	Comforted
Uneasy	Paralyzed	Desperate

_____   _____   _____

I feel as though
I am more _____ about my life.
Relaxed   Excited   Confident

I am _____ with this practice.
Comfortable   Frustrated   Happier

Paying attention to how I feel has helped me to
_____
_____
_____
_____
_____
_____
_____

Be more selfish
Find more balance
Be more patient with others

WHAT OTHERS THINK OF ME IS NONE OF MY BUSINESS.

DAY 39   DATE_____

I APPRECIATE
_____

The emotions I experienced upon awakening were
_____ & _____

Moving Meditations completed
_____
_____

Subjects that came to mind during visualization practice
_____
_____
_____
_____
_____
_____

The three most dominant emotions/
feelings I experienced today were:

Calm	Peaceful	Passionate
Intrigued	Concerned	Comforted
Uneasy	Paralyzed	Desperate
_____	_____	_____

I feel as though
I am more _____ about my life.
Relaxed   Excited   Confident
I am _____ with this practice.
Comfortable   Frustrated   Happier

Paying attention to how I feel has helped me to
_____
_____
_____
_____
_____
_____

Be more selfish
Find more balance
Be more patient with others

PERSEVERANCE.

DAY 40   DATE_____

I APPRECIATE

_____

The emotions I experienced upon awakening were

_____&_____

Moving Meditations completed

_____

_____

Subjects that came to mind during visualization practice

_____
_____
_____
_____
_____

The three most dominant emotions/
feelings I experienced today were:

Calm	Peaceful	Passionate
Intrigued	Concerned	Comforted
Uneasy	Paralyzed	Desperate

_____   _____   _____

I feel as though
I am more _____ about my life.

Relaxed   Excited   Confident

I am _____ with this practice.

Comfortable   Frustrated   Happier

Paying attention to how I feel has helped me to

_____
_____
_____
_____
_____
_____
_____

Be more selfish
Find more balance
Be more patient with others

PEACE OR PANIC?

DAY 41   DATE_____

I APPRECIATE
_____

The emotions I experienced upon awakening were
_____&_____

Moving Meditations completed

_____

_____

Subjects that came to mind during visualization practice
_____
_____
_____
_____

The three most dominant emotions/
feelings I experienced today were:

Calm	Peaceful	Passionate
Intrigued	Concerned	Comforted
Uneasy	Paralyzed	Desperate

_____   _____   _____

I feel as though
I am more _____ about my life.
Relaxed   Excited   Confident

I am _____ with this practice.
Comfortable   Frustrated   Happier

Paying attention to how I feel has helped me to

_____
_____
_____
_____
_____

Be more selfish
Find more balance
Be more patient with others

BECAUSE I BELIEVE, I CELEBRATE IN ADVANCE.

DAY 42   DATE_____

I APPRECIATE
_____
The emotions I experienced upon awakening were
_____ & _____
Moving Meditations completed
_____
_____
Subjects that came to mind during visualization practice
_____
_____
_____
_____
_____

The three most dominant emotions/
feelings I experienced today were:

Calm	Peaceful	Passionate
Intrigued	Concerned	Comforted
Uneasy	Paralyzed	Desperate

_____   _____   _____

I feel as though
I am more _____ about my life.

| Relaxed | Excited | Confident |

I am _____ with this practice.

| Comfortable | Frustrated | Happier |

Paying attention to how I feel has helped me to

_____
_____
_____
_____
_____
_____

Be more selfish
Find more balance
Be more patient with others

I AM A UNIQUE MELODY.

DAY 43   DATE_____

I APPRECIATE

_____

The emotions I experienced upon awakening were

_____ & _____

Moving Meditations completed

_____

_____

Subjects that came to mind during visualization practice

_____

_____

_____

_____

_____

_____

The three most dominant emotions/ feelings I experienced today were:

Calm	Peaceful	Passionate
Intrigued	Concerned	Comforted
Uneasy	Paralyzed	Desperate
_____	_____	_____

I feel as though
I am more _____ about my life.
Relaxed   Excited   Confident

I am _____ with this practice.
Comfortable   Frustrated   Happier

Paying attention to how I feel has helped me to
_____
_____
_____
_____
_____

Be more selfish
Find more balance
Be more patient with others

MY MIND AND BODY ARE IN RHYTHYM.

DAY 44   DATE_____

I APPRECIATE
_____
The emotions I experienced upon awakening were
_____&_____
Moving Meditations completed
_____

_____
Subjects that came to mind during visualization practice
_____
_____
_____
_____
_____

The three most dominant emotions/feelings I experienced today were:

Calm	Peaceful	Passionate
Intrigued	Concerned	Comforted
Uneasy	Paralyzed	Desperate
_____	_____	_____

I feel as though
I am more _____ about my life.
Relaxed   Excited   Confident

I am _____ with this practice.
Comfortable   Frustrated   Happier

Paying attention to how I feel has helped me to
_____
_____
_____
_____
_____
_____
_____

Be more selfish
Find more balance
Be more patient with others

LOVE YOURSELF.

DAY 45 DATE_____

I APPRECIATE
_____

The emotions I experienced upon awakening were
_____ & _____

Moving Meditations completed
_____
_____

Subjects that came to mind during visualization practice
_____
_____
_____
_____

The three most dominant emotions/
feelings I experienced today were:

| Doubtful | Nervous | Affectionate |
| Annoyed | Deprived | Alone |

I feel as though

Paying attention to how I feel has helped me to

THINGS ARE ALWAYS WORKING OUT FOR ME.

DAY 46　　　　　DATE_____

I APPRECIATE

_____

The emotions I experienced upon awakening were

_____ & _____

Moving Meditations completed

_____

_____

Subjects that came to mind during visualization practice

_____
_____
_____
_____
_____
_____

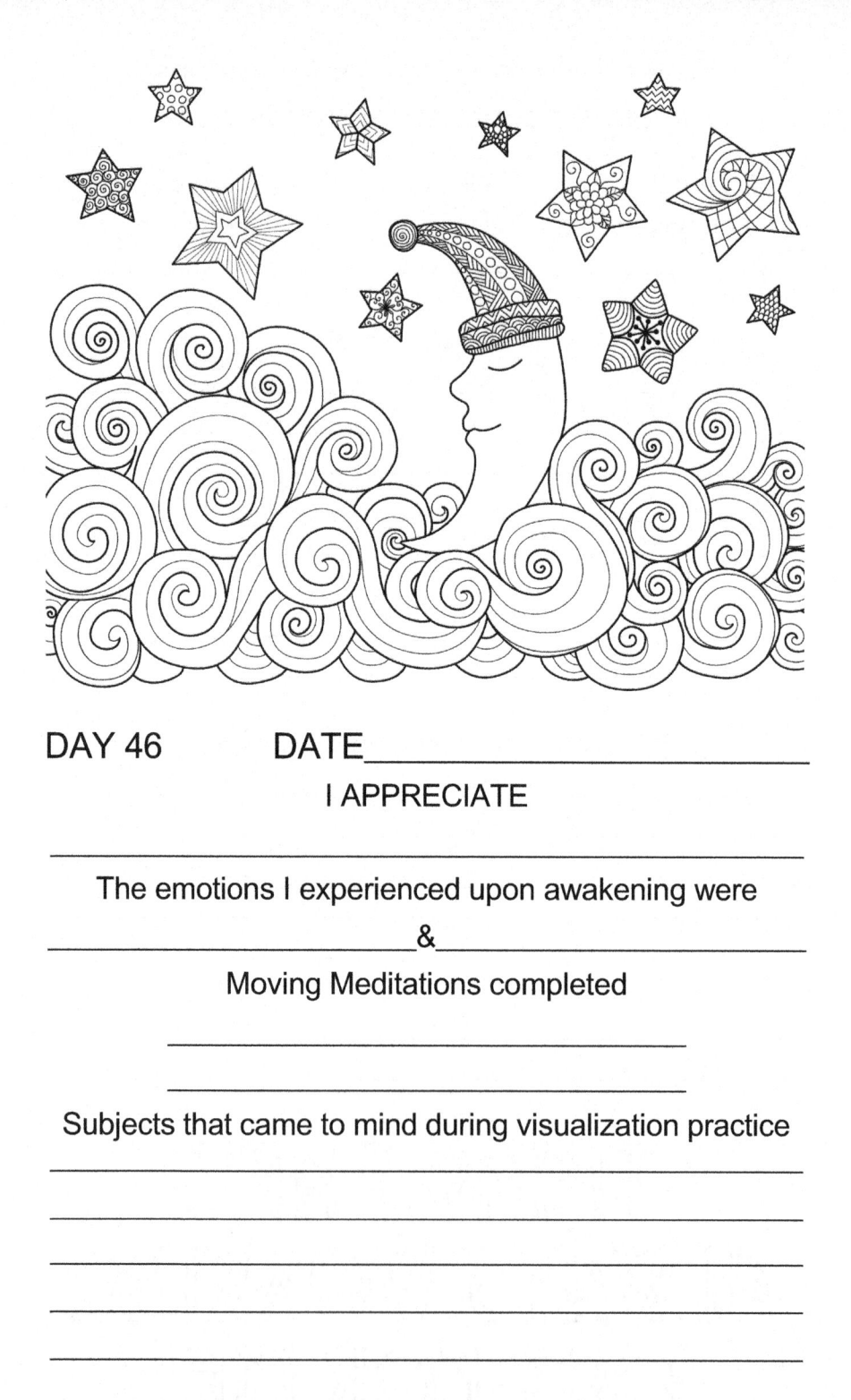

The three most dominant emotions/
feelings I experienced today were:

| Doubtful | Nervous | Affectionate |
| Annoyed | Deprived | Alone |

I feel as though

_____
_____
_____
_____
_____
_____
_____
_____
_____

Paying attention to how I feel has helped me to

_____
_____
_____
_____
_____
_____
_____
_____
_____

I REST AND LISTEN TO MY BODY.

DAY 47   DATE _____

I APPRECIATE

_____

The emotions I experienced upon awakening were
_____ & _____

Moving Meditations completed
_____

_____

Subjects that came to mind during visualization practice
_____
_____
_____
_____

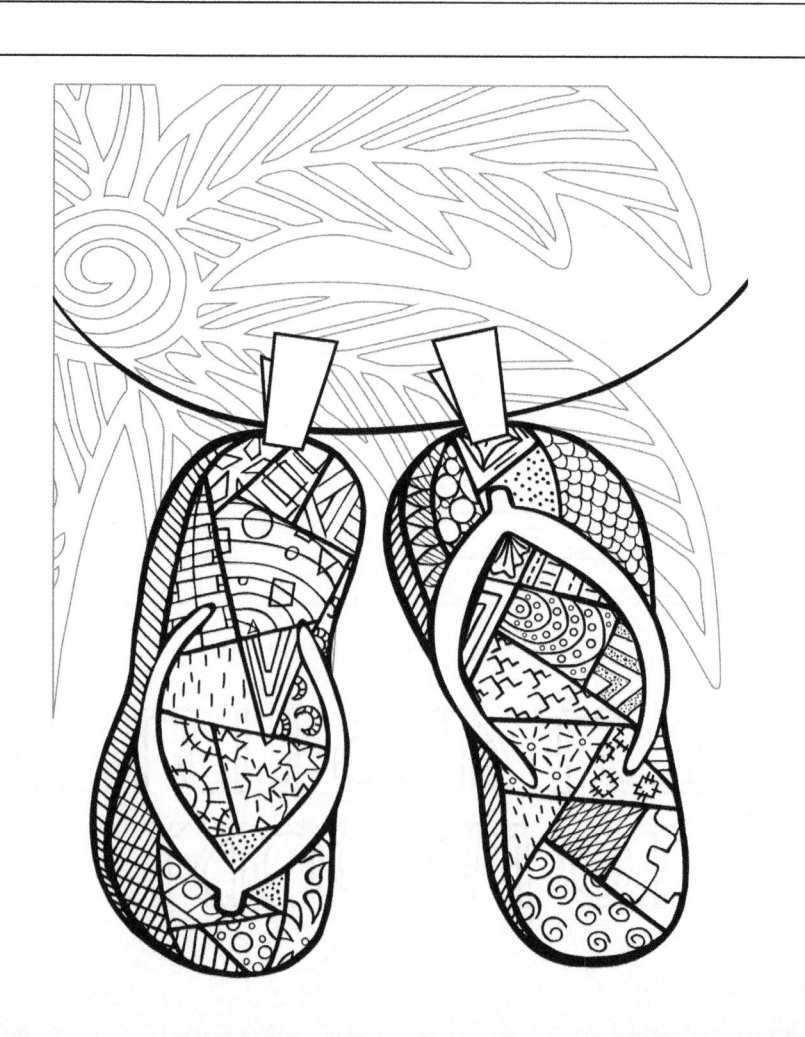

The three most dominant emotions/
feelings I experienced today were:

| Doubtful | Nervous | Affectionate |
| Annoyed | Deprived | Alone |

I feel as though

Paying attention to how I feel has helped me to

DOING NOTHING IS DOING SOMETHING.

DAY 48   DATE_____

I APPRECIATE
_____

The emotions I experienced upon awakening were
_____&_____

Moving Meditations completed
_____
_____

Subjects that came to mind during visualization practice
_____
_____
_____
_____
_____

The three most dominant emotions/
feelings I experienced today were:

| Doubtful | Nervous | Affectionate |
| Annoyed | Deprived | Alone |

I feel as though
_____
_____
_____
_____
_____
_____
_____
_____

Paying attention to how I feel has helped me to
_____
_____
_____
_____
_____
_____
_____
_____

I ALWAYS HAVE ENOUGH TIME.

DAY 49   DATE_____

I APPRECIATE
_____

The emotions I experienced upon awakening were
_____ & _____

Moving Meditations completed
_____
_____

Subjects that came to mind during visualization practice
_____
_____
_____
_____
_____

The three most dominant emotions/
feelings I experienced today were:

| Doubtful | Nervous | Affectionate |
| Annoyed | Deprived | Alone |

_____

I feel as though
_____
_____
_____
_____
_____
_____
_____
_____

Paying attention to how I feel has helped me to
_____
_____
_____
_____
_____
_____
_____
_____

WHAT DO I CHOOSE TO SEE.

DAY 50   DATE_____

I APPRECIATE
_____

The emotions I experienced upon awakening were
_____ & _____

Moving Meditations completed
_____

_____
Subjects that came to mind during visualization practice
_____
_____
_____
_____
_____
_____
_____
_____

The three most dominant emotions/
feelings I experienced today were:

| Doubtful | Nervous | Affectionate |
| Annoyed | Deprived | Alone |

I feel as though

_____
_____
_____
_____
_____
_____
_____
_____
_____

Paying attention to how I feel has helped me to

_____
_____
_____
_____
_____
_____
_____
_____
_____

LIFE IS A WILD RIDE.

DAY 51   DATE_____

I APPRECIATE
_____

The emotions I experienced upon awakening were
_____ & _____

Moving Meditations completed
_____
_____

Subjects that came to mind during visualization practice
_____
_____
_____
_____

The three most dominant emotions/ feelings I experienced today were:

| Doubtful | Nervous | Affectionate |
| Annoyed | Deprived | Alone |

I feel as though

_____
_____
_____
_____
_____
_____
_____
_____
_____

Paying attention to how I feel has helped me to

_____
_____
_____
_____
_____
_____
_____
_____
_____

I ALWAYS LET LOVE WIN.

DAY 52	DATE_____

I APPRECIATE
_____

The emotions I experienced upon awakening were
_____ & _____

Moving Meditations completed
_____
_____

Subjects that came to mind during visualization practice
_____
_____
_____
_____
_____
_____
_____

The three most dominant emotions/
feelings I experienced today were:

| Doubtful | Nervous | Affectionate |
| Annoyed | Deprived | Alone |

I feel as though

_____
_____
_____
_____
_____
_____
_____
_____
_____

Paying attention to how I feel has helped me to

_____
_____
_____
_____
_____
_____
_____
_____
_____

I BELIEVE.

DAY 53   DATE_____

I APPRECIATE

_____

The emotions I experienced upon awakening were

_____ & _____

Moving Meditations completed

_____

_____

Subjects that came to mind during visualization practice

_____

_____

_____

_____

_____

The three most dominant emotions/
feelings I experienced today were:

| Doubtful | Nervous | Affectionate |
| Annoyed | Deprived | Alone |

I feel as though
_____
_____
_____
_____
_____
_____
_____
_____
_____
_____

Paying attention to how I feel has helped me to
_____
_____
_____
_____
_____
_____
_____
_____

I DON'T WANT CONTROL, I WANT TO LET GO.

DAY 54   DATE_____

I APPRECIATE
_____
The emotions I experienced upon awakening were
_____ & _____
Moving Meditations completed
_____
_____
Subjects that came to mind during visualization practice
_____
_____
_____
_____
_____
_____

The three most dominant emotions/
feelings I experienced today were:

| Doubtful | Nervous | Affectionate |
| Annoyed | Deprived | Alone |

I feel as though

_____
_____
_____
_____
_____
_____
_____
_____

Paying attention to how I feel has helped me to

_____
_____
_____
_____
_____
_____
_____
_____

EVERY LITTLE THING IS GONNA BE ALRIGHT.

DAY 55   DATE_____

I APPRECIATE

_____

The emotions I experienced upon awakening were
_____ & _____

Moving Meditations completed
_____
_____

Subjects that came to mind during visualization practice
_____
_____
_____
_____
_____

The three most dominant emotions/
feelings I experienced today were:

| Doubtful | Nervous | Affectionate |
| Annoyed | Deprived | Alone |

I feel as though
_____
_____
_____
_____
_____
_____
_____
_____
_____

Paying attention to how I feel has helped me to
_____
_____
_____
_____
_____
_____
_____
_____
_____

EVERY DAY, I TRY TO SPEND A LITTLE TIME OUTSIDE.

DAY 56   DATE_____

I APPRECIATE
_____
The emotions I experienced upon awakening were
_____&_____
Moving Meditations completed
_____
_____
Subjects that came to mind during visualization practice
_____
_____
_____
_____
_____
_____

The three most dominant emotions/
feelings I experienced today were:

| Doubtful | Nervous | Affectionate |
| Annoyed | Deprived | Alone |

I feel as though

_____
_____
_____
_____
_____
_____
_____
_____
_____

Paying attention to how I feel has helped me to

_____
_____
_____
_____
_____
_____
_____
_____
_____

I AM STRONGER THAN I KNOW.

DAY 57   DATE_____

I APPRECIATE
_____

The emotions I experienced upon awakening were
_____ & _____

Moving Meditations completed
_____
_____

Subjects that came to mind during visualization practice
_____
_____
_____
_____
_____

The three most dominant emotions/
feelings I experienced today were:

| Doubtful | Nervous | Affectionate |
| Annoyed | Deprived | Alone |

I feel as though
_____
_____
_____
_____
_____
_____
_____
_____

Paying attention to how I feel has helped me to
_____
_____
_____
_____
_____
_____
_____
_____

AIM FOR YOUR DESIRES AND TRUST THE UNIVERSE.

DAY 58   DATE_____

I APPRECIATE
_____

The emotions I experienced upon awakening were
_____&_____
Moving Meditations completed
_____
_____

Subjects that came to mind during visualization practice
_____
_____
_____
_____
_____
_____

The three most dominant emotions/
feelings I experienced today were:

| Doubtful | Nervous | Affectionate |
| Annoyed | Deprived | Alone |

I feel as though
_____
_____
_____
_____
_____
_____
_____
_____

Paying attention to how I feel has helped me to
_____
_____
_____
_____
_____
_____
_____
_____

LIFE IS GOOD.

DAY 59   DATE_____

I APPRECIATE
_____

The emotions I experienced upon awakening were
_____ & _____

Moving Meditations completed
_____
_____

Subjects that came to mind during visualization practice
_____
_____
_____
_____
_____
_____

The three most dominant emotions/
feelings I experienced today were:

| Doubtful | Nervous | Affectionate |
| Annoyed | Deprived | Alone |

I feel as though

_____
_____
_____
_____
_____
_____
_____
_____

Paying attention to how I feel has helped me to

_____
_____
_____
_____
_____
_____
_____
_____

JUST KEEP SWIMMING.

DAY 60   DATE _____

I APPRECIATE

_____
The emotions I experienced upon awakening were
_____ & _____
Moving Meditations completed
    _____
    _____

Subjects that came to mind during visualization practice
_____
_____
_____
_____
_____

The three most dominant emotions/
feelings I experienced today were:

| Doubtful | Nervous | Affectionate |
| Annoyed | Deprived | Alone |

I feel as though

_____
_____
_____
_____
_____
_____
_____
_____

Paying attention to how I feel has helped me to

_____
_____
_____
_____
_____
_____
_____
_____

MY MIND AND BODY SERVE ME WELL.

DAY 61

DATE_____

TODAY I FEEL APPRECIATION FOR
_____
_____

THE EMOTIONS I EXPERIENCED UPON AWAKENING WERE
_____ & _____.
MOVING MEDITATIONS COMPLETED
_____

MOVING FORWARD I WILL USE MY VISUALIZATION TIME EACH MORNING TO IDENTIFY THE GAPS BETWEEN WHERE I AM AND WHERE I WANT TO BE. THIS WILL HELP ME TO SHIFT MORE QUICKLY TOWARD MY DESIRES. I WILL BE QUICK TO USE MY MOVING MEDITATION PRACTICE. IT IS A POWERFUL TOOL THAT I CAN RELY ON TO ASSIST ME IN THIS PRACTICE OF SHIFTING AND CLOSING THE GAPS.

_____
_____
_____
_____
_____
_____
_____
_____
_____
_____

The three most dominant emotions/
feelings I experienced today were:

Suspicious   Playful   Offended
Admired   Stressed   Prosperous
_____   _____   _____

I feel as though
Now that I am clear that nothing is more important than
that I feel good, _____
I feel less guilty   I sleep better   I am more content
I am certain I am making a difference
I find it easier to commit to a physical practice
I worry less about what I can't control
I encourage others to do so as well
It's easier to embrace the contrast

Music helps me to _____.
Quiet my mind   Shift more easily   Become more creative
Release emotions   Find relief   Live in more Joy

Moving Meditations_____
It helped me to _____
_____

I LOVE ME TO INFINITY AND BEYOND.

DAY 62

DATE _____

TODAY I FEEL APPRECIATION FOR

_____
_____

THE EMOTIONS I EXPERIENCED UPON AWAKENING WERE

_____
& _____.

MOVING MEDITATIONS COMPLETED

_____

VISUALIZATION/SHIFTING/GAPS

_____
_____
_____

The three most dominant emotions/
feelings I experienced today were:

Suspicious   Playful   Offended
Admired   Stressed   Prosperous
_____   _____   _____

I feel as though
Now that I am clear that nothing is more important than that I feel good, _____
I feel less guilty   I sleep better   I am more content
I am certain I am making a difference
I find it easier to commit to a physical practice
I worry less about what I can't control
I encourage others to do so as well
It's easier to embrace the contrast

Music helps me to _____.
Quiet my mind   Shift more easily   Become more creative
Release emotions   Find relief   Live in more Joy

Moving Meditations _____
It helped me to _____
_____

I AM FLEXIBLE WITH MY THOUGHTS.

DAY 63

DATE _____

TODAY I FEEL APPRECIATION FOR

_____

_____

THE EMOTIONS I EXPERIENCED UPON AWAKENING WERE

_____

& _____ .

MOVING MEDITATIONS COMPLETED

_____

VISUALIZATION/SHIFTING/GAPS

_____

_____

_____

_____

The three most dominant emotions/
feelings I experienced today were:

Suspicious   Playful   Offended
Admired   Stressed   Prosperous
_____   _____   _____

I feel as though
Now that I am clear that nothing is more important than
that I feel good, _____
I feel less guilty   I sleep better   I am more content
I am certain I am making a difference
I find it easier to commit to a physical practice
I worry less about what I can't control
I encourage others to do so as well
It's easier to embrace the contrast

Music helps me to _____.
Quiet my mind   Shift more easily   Become more creative
Release emotions   Find relief   Live in more Joy

Moving Meditations _____
It helped me to _____
_____

I AM A GREAT COMMUNICATOR.

DAY 64

DATE _____

TODAY I FEEL APPRECIATION FOR
_____
_____

THE EMOTIONS I EXPERIENCED UPON AWAKENING WERE
_____
& _____.

MOVING MEDITATIONS COMPLETED
_____

VISUALIZATION/SHIFTING/GAPS
_____
_____
_____
_____

The three most dominant emotions/feelings I experienced today were:

Suspicious   Playful   Offended
Admired   Stressed   Prosperous

_____   _____   _____

I feel as though
Now that I am clear that nothing is more important than that I feel good, _____
I feel less guilty   I sleep better   I am more content
I am certain I am making a difference
I find it easier to commit to a physical practice
I worry less about what I can't control
I encourage others to do so as well
It's easier to embrace the contrast

Music helps me to _____.
Quiet my mind   Shift more easily   Become more creative
Release emotions   Find relief   Live in more Joy

Moving Meditations _____
It helped me to _____
_____

NO JUDGMENT.

DAY 65

DATE _____

TODAY I FEEL APPRECIATION FOR
_____
_____

THE EMOTIONS I EXPERIENCED UPON AWAKENING WERE
_____
& _____.

MOVING MEDITATIONS COMPLETED
_____

VISUALIZATION/SHIFTING/GAPS
_____
_____
_____
_____

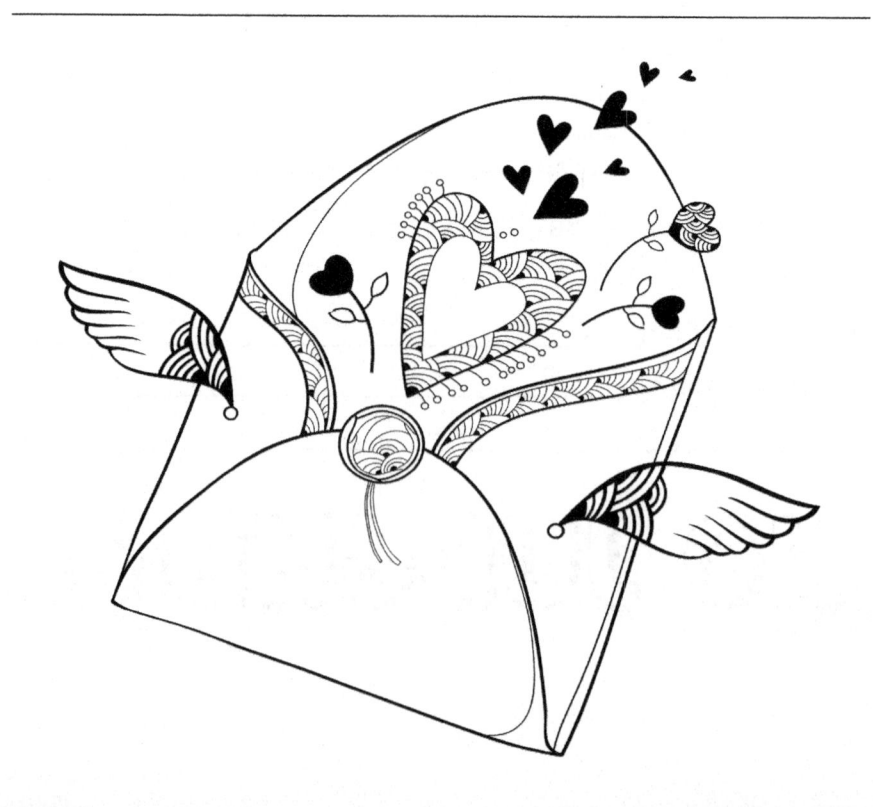

The three most dominant emotions/feelings I experienced today were:

Suspicious   Playful   Offended
Admired   Stressed   Prosperous

_____   _____   _____

I feel as though
Now that I am clear that nothing is more important than that I feel good, _____
I feel less guilty   I sleep better   I am more content
I am certain I am making a difference
I find it easier to commit to a physical practice
I worry less about what I can't control
I encourage others to do so as well
It's easier to embrace the contrast

Music helps me to _____.
Quiet my mind   Shift more easily   Become more creative
Release emotions   Find relief   Live in more Joy

Moving Meditations _____
It helped me to _____
_____

I CHOOSE LOVE.

DAY 66

DATE _____

TODAY I FEEL APPRECIATION FOR
_____
_____

THE EMOTIONS I EXPERIENCED UPON AWAKENING WERE
_____
& _____.

MOVING MEDITATIONS COMPLETED
_____

VISUALIZATION/SHIFTING/GAPS
_____
_____
_____
_____

The three most dominant emotions/
feelings I experienced today were:

Suspicious Playful   Offended
Admired   Stressed   Prosperous
_____   _____   _____

I feel as though
Now that I am clear that nothing is more important than
that I feel good, _____
I feel less guilty   I sleep better   I am more content
I am certain I am making a difference
I find it easier to commit to a physical practice
I worry less about what I can't control
I encourage others to do so as well
It's easier to embrace the contrast

Music helps me to _____.
Quiet my mind   Shift more easily   Become more creative
Release emotions   Find relief   Live in more Joy

Moving Meditations _____
It helped me to _____
_____

I LOVE TO LEARN.

DAY 67

DATE _____

TODAY I FEEL APPRECIATION FOR

_____

_____

THE EMOTIONS I EXPERIENCED UPON AWAKENING WERE

_____

& _____.

MOVING MEDITATIONS COMPLETED

_____

VISUALIZATION/SHIFTING/GAPS

_____

_____

_____

_____

The three most dominant emotions/
feelings I experienced today were:

Suspicious Playful   Offended
Admired   Stressed   Prosperous
_____   _____   _____

I feel as though
Now that I am clear that nothing is more important than
that I feel good, _____
I feel less guilty   I sleep better   I am more content
I am certain I am making a difference
I find it easier to commit to a physical practice
I worry less about what I can't control
I encourage others to do so as well
It's easier to embrace the contrast

Music helps me to _____.
Quiet my mind   Shift more easily   Become more creative
Release emotions   Find relief   Live in more Joy

Moving Meditations _____
It helped me to _____
_____

SOMETIMES IT'S GOOD TO LET GO AND SAIL AWAY.

DAY 68

DATE _____

TODAY I FEEL APPRECIATION FOR

_____

_____

THE EMOTIONS I EXPERIENCED UPON AWAKENING WERE

_____

& _____.

MOVING MEDITATIONS COMPLETED

_____

VISUALIZATION/SHIFTING/GAPS

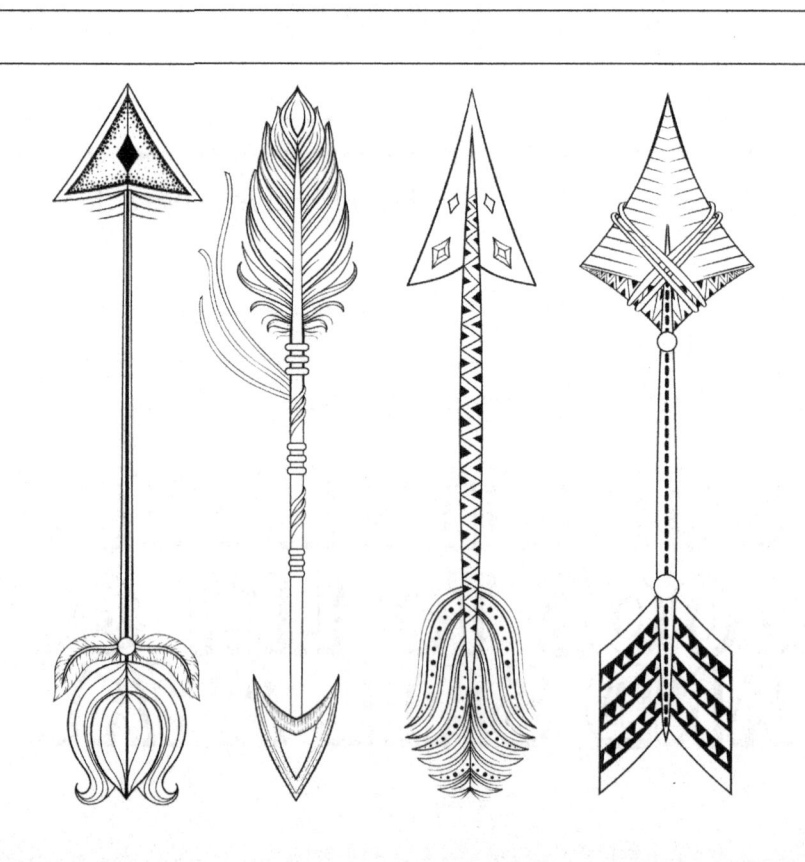

_____

_____

_____

_____

The three most dominant emotions/
feelings I experienced today were:

Suspicious Playful   Offended
Admired   Stressed   Prosperous
_____   _____   _____

I feel as though
Now that I am clear that nothing is more important than
that I feel good, _____
I feel less guilty   I sleep better   I am more content
I am certain I am making a difference
I find it easier to commit to a physical practice
I worry less about what I can't control
I encourage others to do so as well
It's easier to embrace the contrast

Music helps me to _____.
Quiet my mind   Shift more easily   Become more creative
Release emotions   Find relief   Live in more Joy

Moving Meditations _____
It helped me to _____
_____

I AIM AND LET GO.

DAY 69

DATE _____

TODAY I FEEL APPRECIATION FOR
_____
_____

THE EMOTIONS I EXPERIENCED UPON AWAKENING WERE
_____
& _____.

MOVING MEDITATIONS COMPLETED
_____

VISUALIZATION/SHIFTING/GAPS
_____
_____
_____

The three most dominant emotions/feelings I experienced today were:

Suspicious   Playful   Offended
Admired   Stressed   Prosperous
_____   _____   _____

I feel as though
Now that I am clear that nothing is more important than that I feel good, _____
I feel less guilty   I sleep better   I am more content
I am certain I am making a difference
I find it easier to commit to a physical practice
I worry less about what I can't control
I encourage others to do so as well
It's easier to embrace the contrast

Music helps me to _____.
Quiet my mind   Shift more easily   Become more creative
Release emotions   Find relief   Live in more Joy

Moving Meditations _____
It helped me to _____
_____

SOMETIMES IT'S EASIER TO MEET IN THE MIDDLE.

DAY 70

DATE _____

TODAY I FEEL APPRECIATION FOR
_____
_____

THE EMOTIONS I EXPERIENCED UPON AWAKENING WERE
_____
& _____.

MOVING MEDITATIONS COMPLETED
_____

VISUALIZATION/SHIFTING/GAPS
_____
_____
_____
_____

The three most dominant emotions/
feelings I experienced today were:

Suspicious   Playful   Offended
Admired   Stressed   Prosperous
_____   _____   _____

I feel as though
Now that I am clear that nothing is more important than
that I feel good, _____
I feel less guilty   I sleep better   I am more content
I am certain I am making a difference
I find it easier to commit to a physical practice
I worry less about what I can't control
I encourage others to do so as well
It's easier to embrace the contrast

Music helps me to _____.
Quiet my mind   Shift more easily   Become more creative
Release emotions   Find relief   Live in more Joy

Moving Meditations _____
_____

TEATIME EQUALS ME TIME.

DAY 71

DATE _____

TODAY I FEEL APPRECIATION FOR
_____
_____

THE EMOTIONS I EXPERIENCED UPON AWAKENING WERE
_____
& _____.

MOVING MEDITATIONS COMPLETED
_____

VISUALIZATION/SHIFTING/GAPS
_____
_____
_____
_____

The three most dominant emotions/
feelings I experienced today were:

Suspicious Playful   Offended
Admired   Stressed   Prosperous
_____   _____   _____

I feel as though
Now that I am clear that nothing is more important than
that I feel good, _____
I feel less guilty   I sleep better   I am more content
I am certain I am making a difference
I find it easier to commit to a physical practice
I worry less about what I can't control
I encourage others to do so as well
It's easier to embrace the contrast

Music helps me to _____.
Quiet my mind   Shift more easily   Become more creative
Release emotions   Find relief   Live in more Joy

Moving Meditations _____
It helped me to _____
_____

NOW IS THE TIME TO CONNECT WITH NATURE.

DAY 72

DATE _____

TODAY I FEEL APPRECIATION FOR

_____

_____

THE EMOTIONS I EXPERIENCED UPON AWAKENING WERE

_____

& _____ .

MOVING MEDITATIONS COMPLETED

_____

VISUALIZATION/SHIFTING/GAPS

_____

_____

_____

_____

The three most dominant emotions/
feelings I experienced today were:

Suspicious Playful   Offended
Admired   Stressed   Prosperous
_____   _____   _____

I feel as though
Now that I am clear that nothing is more important than that I feel good, _____
I feel less guilty   I sleep better   I am more content
I am certain I am making a difference
I find it easier to commit to a physical practice
I worry less about what I can't control
I encourage others to do so as well
It's easier to embrace the contrast

Music helps me to _____.
Quiet my mind   Shift more easily   Become more creative
Release emotions   Find relief   Live in more Joy

Moving Meditations _____
It helped me to _____
_____

I HAVE ALL THE ENERGY I NEED.

DAY 73

DATE _____

TODAY I FEEL APPRECIATION FOR
_____
_____

THE EMOTIONS I EXPERIENCED UPON
AWAKENING WERE
_____
& _____.

MOVING MEDITATIONS COMPLETED
_____

VISUALIZATION/SHIFTING/GAPS
_____
_____
_____

The three most dominant emotions/
feelings I experienced today were:

Suspicious Playful   Offended
Admired   Stressed   Prosperous
_____   _____   _____

I feel as though
Now that I am clear that nothing is more important than
that I feel good, _____
I feel less guilty   I sleep better   I am more content
I am certain I am making a difference
I find it easier to commit to a physical practice
I worry less about what I can't control
I encourage others to do so as well
It's easier to embrace the contrast

Music helps me to _____.
Quiet my mind   Shift more easily   Become more creative
Release emotions   Find relief   Live in more Joy

Moving Meditations _____
It helped me to _____
_____

MY WARRIOR TRIBE IS MY FAMILY.

DAY 74

DATE _____

TODAY I FEEL APPRECIATION FOR

_____

_____

THE EMOTIONS I EXPERIENCED UPON AWAKENING WERE

_____

& _____.

MOVING MEDITATIONS COMPLETED

_____

VISUALIZATION/SHIFTING/GAPS

_____

_____

_____

The three most dominant emotions/feelings I experienced today were:

Suspicious   Playful   Offended
Admired   Stressed   Prosperous

_____   _____   _____

I feel as though
Now that I am clear that nothing is more important than that I feel good, _____
I feel less guilty   I sleep better   I am more content
I am certain I am making a difference
I find it easier to commit to a physical practice
I worry less about what I can't control
I encourage others to do so as well
It's easier to embrace the contrast

Music helps me to _____.
Quiet my mind   Shift more easily   Become more creative
Release emotions   Find relief   Live in more Joy

Moving Meditations _____
It helped me to _____
_____

I LOVE TRYING NEW THINGS.

DAY 75

DATE _____

TODAY I FEEL APPRECIATION FOR

_____

_____

THE EMOTIONS I EXPERIENCED UPON AWAKENING WERE

_____

& _____ .

MOVING MEDITATIONS COMPLETED

_____

VISUALIZATION/SHIFTING/GAPS

_____

_____

_____

The three most dominant emotions/feelings I experienced today were:

Suspicious   Playful   Offended
Admired   Stressed   Prosperous

_____   _____   _____

I feel as though
Now that I am clear that nothing is more important than that I feel good, _____
I feel less guilty   I sleep better   I am more content
I am certain I am making a difference
I find it easier to commit to a physical practice
I worry less about what I can't control
I encourage others to do so as well
It's easier to embrace the contrast

Music helps me to _____.
Quiet my mind   Shift more easily   Become more creative
Release emotions   Find relief   Live in more Joy

Moving Meditations _____
It helped me to _____
_____

I LOVE TO HANG OUT AND CONNECT.

DAY 76

DATE _____

TODAY I FEEL APPRECIATION FOR
_____
_____

THE EMOTIONS I EXPERIENCED UPON AWAKENING WERE
_____
& _____.

MOVING MEDITATIONS COMPLETED
_____

VISUALIZATION/SHIFTING/GAPS
_____
_____
_____
_____

The three most dominant emotions/ feelings I experienced today were:

Absorbed   Bitter   Frightened
Considerate   Free   Powerful
_____   _____   _____

I feel:
_____
_____
_____
_____
_____
_____

Shifting:
_____helps me to
_____
_____
_____
_____

Moving Meditation for today_____.
Today I will begin identifying what my "word" is. I am now able to articulate what I am feeling at any given moment.
My Word for today_____.

DIFFERENT IS GOOD.

DAY 77

DATE _____

TODAY I FEEL APPRECIATION FOR
_____
_____

THE EMOTIONS I EXPERIENCED UPON AWAKENING WERE
_____
& _____.

MOVING MEDITATIONS COMPLETED
_____

VISUALIZATION/SHIFTING/GAPS
_____
_____
_____

The three most dominant emotions/
feelings I experienced today were:

| Absorbed | Bitter | Frightened |
| Considerate | Free | Powerful |

_____ _____ _____

I feel:
_____
_____
_____
_____
_____
_____
_____
_____

Shifting:
_____helps me to
_____
_____
_____

Moving Meditation for today_____.
My Word for today_____.

I TAKE LIFE ONE STEP AT A TIME.

DAY 78

DATE _____

TODAY I FEEL APPRECIATION FOR
_____
_____

THE EMOTIONS I EXPERIENCED UPON AWAKENING WERE
_____
& _____.

MOVING MEDITATIONS COMPLETED
_____

VISUALIZATION/SHIFTING/GAPS
_____
_____
_____
_____

The three most dominant emotions/
feelings I experienced today were:

Absorbed   Bitter   Frightened
Considerate   Free   Powerful
_____   _____   _____

I feel:
_____
_____
_____
_____
_____
_____

Shifting:
_____ helps me to
_____
_____
_____

Moving Meditation for today_____.
My word for today_____.

FRIENDS COME IN ALL SHAPES AND SIZES.

DAY 79

DATE _____

TODAY I FEEL APPRECIATION FOR

_____

_____

THE EMOTIONS I EXPERIENCED UPON AWAKENING WERE

_____

& _____.

MOVING MEDITATIONS COMPLETED

_____

VISUALIZATION/SHIFTING/GAPS

_____

_____

_____

The three most dominant emotions/
feelings I experienced today were:

Absorbed	Bitter	Frightened
Considerate	Free	Powerful
_____	_____	_____

I feel:
_____
_____
_____
_____
_____
_____
_____

Shifting:
_____ helps me to
_____
_____
_____

Moving Meditation for today_____.
My Word for today_____.

I PAY ATTENTION TO MY PATTERNS.

DAY 80

DATE _____

TODAY I FEEL APPRECIATION FOR
_____
_____

THE EMOTIONS I EXPERIENCED UPON
AWAKENING WERE
_____
& _____.

MOVING MEDITATIONS COMPLETED
_____

VISUALIZATION/SHIFTING/GAPS
_____
_____
_____
_____

The three most dominant emotions/
feelings I experienced today were:

Absorbed   Bitter   Frightened
Considerate   Free   Powerful
_____   _____   _____

I feel:
_____
_____
_____
_____
_____
_____
_____

Shifting:
_____helps me to
_____
_____
_____
_____

Moving Meditation for today_____.
My Word for today_____.

MY SPACE IS MY SANCTUARY.

DAY 81

DATE _____

TODAY I FEEL APPRECIATION FOR
_____
_____

THE EMOTIONS I EXPERIENCED UPON AWAKENING WERE
_____
& _____.

MOVING MEDITATIONS COMPLETED
_____

VISUALIZATION/SHIFTING/GAPS
_____
_____
_____
_____

The three most dominant emotions/
feelings I experienced today were:

Absorbed   Bitter   Frightened
Considerate   Free   Powerful
_____   _____   _____

I feel:
_____
_____
_____
_____
_____
_____

Shifting:
_____helps me to
_____
_____
_____

Moving Meditation for today_____.
My Word for today_____.

I GIVE MY SOUL PERMISSION TO SHINE.

DAY 82

DATE _____

TODAY I FEEL APPRECIATION FOR

_____

_____

THE EMOTIONS I EXPERIENCED UPON AWAKENING WERE

_____

& _____.

MOVING MEDITATIONS COMPLETED

_____

VISUALIZATION/SHIFTING/GAPS

_____

_____

_____

_____

The three most dominant emotions/
feelings I experienced today were:

Absorbed	Bitter	Frightened
Considerate	Free	Powerful
_____	_____	_____

I feel:
_____
_____
_____
_____
_____
_____
_____

Shifting:
_____ helps me to
_____
_____
_____

Moving Meditation for today_____.
My Word for today_____.

MY THOUGHTS CREATE MY BELIEFS.

DAY 83

DATE _____

TODAY I FEEL APPRECIATION FOR

_____

_____

THE EMOTIONS I EXPERIENCED UPON AWAKENING WERE

_____

& _____.

MOVING MEDITATIONS COMPLETED

_____

VISUALIZATION/SHIFTING/GAPS

_____

_____

_____

The three most dominant emotions/
feelings I experienced today were:

Absorbed	Bitter	Frightened
Considerate	Free	Powerful
_____	_____	_____

I feel:
_____
_____
_____
_____
_____
_____

Shifting:
_____helps me to
_____
_____
_____

Moving Meditation for today_____.
My word for today_____.

I MAKE SLEEP A PRIORITY.

DAY 84

DATE _____

TODAY I FEEL APPRECIATION FOR
_____
_____

THE EMOTIONS I EXPERIENCED UPON AWAKENING WERE
_____
& _____.

MOVING MEDITATIONS COMPLETED
_____

VISUALIZATION/SHIFTING/GAPS
_____
_____
_____
_____

The three most dominant emotions/feelings I experienced today were:

Absorbed   Bitter   Frightened
Considerate   Free   Powerful
_____   _____   _____

I feel:
_____
_____
_____
_____
_____
_____
_____

Shifting:
_____helps me to
_____
_____
_____
_____

Moving Meditation for today_____.
My Word for today_____.

FREEDOM IS A HUMAN RIGHT.

DAY 85

DATE _____

TODAY I FEEL APPRECIATION FOR
_____
_____

THE EMOTIONS I EXPERIENCED UPON AWAKENING WERE
_____
& _____ .

MOVING MEDITATIONS COMPLETED
_____

VISUALIZATION/SHIFTING/GAPS
_____
_____
_____
_____

The three most dominant emotions/
feelings I experienced today were:

Absorbed   Bitter   Frightened
Considerate   Free   Powerful
_____   _____   _____

I feel:
_____
_____
_____
_____
_____
_____
_____

Shifting:
_____helps me to
_____
_____
_____

Moving Meditation for today_____.
My Word for today_____.

WHO'S DRIVIN' MY LIFE?

DAY 86

DATE _____

TODAY I FEEL APPRECIATION FOR
_____
_____

THE EMOTIONS I EXPERIENCED UPON AWAKENING WERE
_____
& _____ .

MOVING MEDITATIONS COMPLETED
_____

VISUALIZATION/SHIFTING/GAPS
_____
_____
_____
_____

Love

The three most dominant emotions/
feelings I experienced today were:

Absorbed	Bitter	Frightened
Considerate	Free	Powerful
_____	_____	_____

I feel:
_____
_____
_____
_____
_____
_____
_____

Shifting:
_____helps me to
_____
_____
_____

Moving Meditation for today_____.
My Word for today_____.

LOVE IS IN THE AIR.

DAY 87

DATE _____

TODAY I FEEL APPRECIATION FOR

_____

_____

THE EMOTIONS I EXPERIENCED UPON AWAKENING WERE

_____

& _____.

MOVING MEDITATIONS COMPLETED

_____

VISUALIZATION/SHIFTING/GAPS

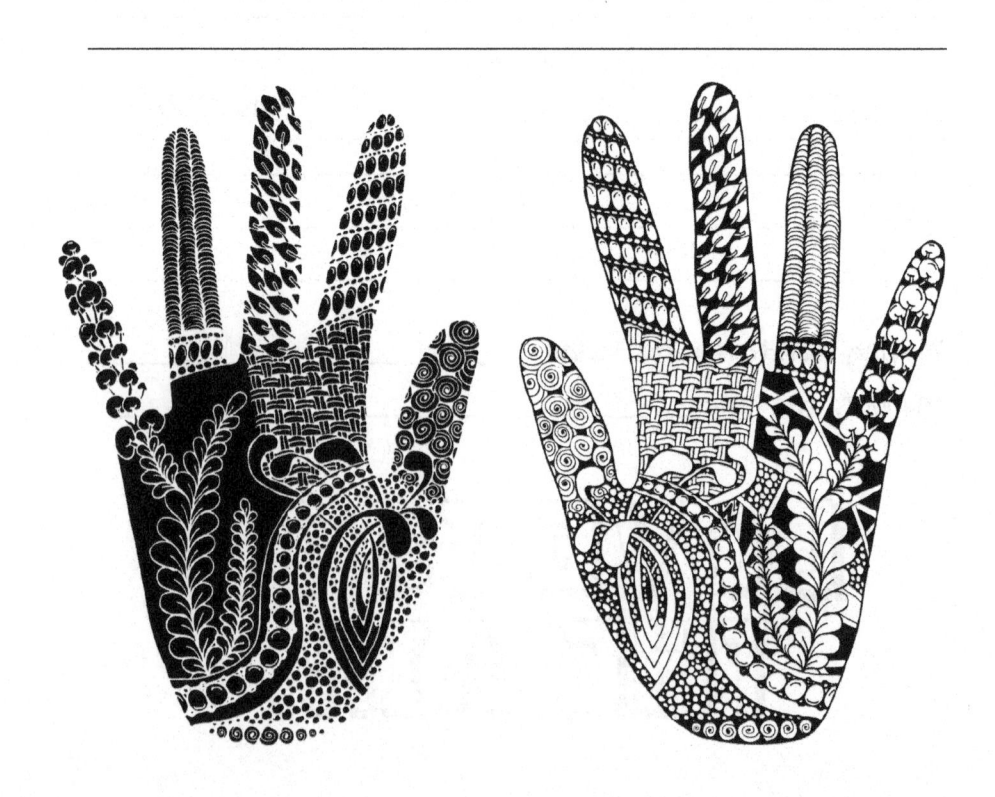

_____
_____
_____
_____

The three most dominant emotions/
feelings I experienced today were:

Absorbed   Bitter   Frightened
Considerate   Free   Powerful
_____   _____   _____

I feel:
_____
_____
_____
_____
_____
_____
_____

Shifting:
_____helps me to
_____
_____
_____

Moving Meditation for today_____.
My Word for today_____.

EVERYTHING I TOUCH BECOMES PART OF MY EXPERIENCE.

DAY 88

DATE _____

TODAY I FEEL APPRECIATION FOR

_____

_____

THE EMOTIONS I EXPERIENCED UPON AWAKENING WERE

_____

& _____.

MOVING MEDITATIONS COMPLETED

_____

VISUALIZATION/SHIFTING/GAPS

_____
_____
_____
_____

The three most dominant emotions/feelings I experienced today were:

Absorbed   Bitter   Frightened
Considerate   Free   Powerful
_____   _____   _____

I feel:
_____
_____
_____
_____
_____
_____

Shifting:
_____helps me to
_____
_____
_____
_____

Moving Meditation for today_____.
My Word for today_____.

THERE'S NO NEED TO BE IN A HURRY.

DAY 89

DATE _____

TODAY I FEEL APPRECIATION FOR
_____
_____

THE EMOTIONS I EXPERIENCED UPON AWAKENING WERE
_____
& _____.

MOVING MEDITATIONS COMPLETED
_____

VISUALIZATION/SHIFTING/GAPS
_____
_____
_____
_____

The three most dominant emotions/feelings I experienced today were:

Absorbed	Bitter	Frightened
Considerate	Free	Powerful
_____	_____	_____

I feel:
_____
_____
_____
_____
_____
_____

Shifting:
_____ helps me to
_____
_____
_____

Moving Meditation for today_____.
My Word for today_____.

MY LIFE IS SHOWERED IN PROSPERITY.

DAY 90

DATE _____

TODAY I FEEL APPRECIATION FOR

_____

_____

THE EMOTIONS I EXPERIENCED UPON AWAKENING WERE

_____

& _____.

MOVING MEDITATIONS COMPLETED

_____

VISUALIZATION/SHIFTING/GAPS

_____

_____

_____

The three most dominant emotions/
feelings I experienced today were:

Absorbed	Bitter	Frightened
Considerate	Free	Powerful
_____	_____	_____

I feel:
_____
_____
_____
_____
_____
_____

Shifting:
_____helps me to
_____
_____
_____

Moving Meditation for today_____.
My word for today_____.

MY MIND ALLOWS ME TO ESCAPE.

Nothing is more important than that I feel good!

Dear Self,

I understand that paying attention to how I feel is essential to my well-being. I am always evolving, learning and growing. Identifying how I feel is my work. I am shifting.

I will continue this self-care practice knowing that consistency is key.

I have begun identifying what I want. There are many things. As I quiet my mind and identify my desires, I can begin to close the gaps between where I am and where I want to be.

This is the beginning of my new story. I appreciate this practice. I respect it. It is **essential**.

As a Warrior, I am knowing that life is supposed to be good for me. And while I may sometimes doubt myself, my heart knows my truth. I am worthy. I am deserving of my desires. It may take some time, but I am getting there.

I have begun connecting with my tribe. I am grateful for our powerful connection.

I will frequently remind myself to be easy about this practice and enjoy the ride.

I will smile more, worry less and live in my Truth. I am ready for Volume II of My Story.

All is well,

Me

List of FEELINGS/EMOTIONS to get you started

Angry, Approval, Annoyed, Afraid, Awkward, Affectionate, Anxious, Alarmed, Awed, Aggravated, Assured, Awake, Amazed, Astonished, Amused, Apprehensive, Absorbed, Appreciated, Ashamed, Accepted, Able, Addled, Admired, Admirable, Affable, Agreeable, Aggressive, Abandoned

Brave, Bothered, Bewildered, Bitter, Bashful, Blue, Baffled, Blissful, Buoyant, Bereaved, Bold

Cheerful, Cooperative, Courageous, Confident, Calm, Cold, Curious, Content, Considerate, Committed, Cautious, Contrast, Cranky, Crestfallen, Contrite, Connected, Chagrined, Carefree, Celebration, Composed, Capable, Caring, Careful, Contemptuous, Cross, Concerned, Complacent, Charitable, Crushed, Compassionate

Defiant, Depressed, Discouraged, Delighted, Disgusted, Determined, Disappointed, Detached, Daring, Disillusioned, Devious, Dismayed, Disenchanted, Doubtful, Distant, Disinterested, Disdainful, Dismissive, Dejected, Disengaged,

Elated, Enthusiastic, Embarrassed, Edgy, Excited, Envious, Exhausted, Eager, Exuberant, Empowered, Enraged, Euphoric, Extravagant, Ecstatic, Eager, Emboldened

Funny, Frightened, Fearful, Free, Freedom, Furious, Fair, Foolish, Frustrated, Forgiving, Forgiven, Fulfilled, Fatigued,

Grouchy, Guilty, Grief-stricken, Generous, Greedy, Grateful, Grumpy, Guarded, Gleeful, Glad, Gloomy, Glum, Gracious

Happy, Humiliated, Hopeful, Hurt, Helpless, Hopeless, Healed Horrified, Hesitant, Humbled, Heartbroken, Hysterical, Hyper

Irritated, Irritable, Interested, Insecure, Impatient, Inspired, Inspiring, Inadequate, Irrational, Ignorant, Indifferent, Irked, Impertinent, Inquisitive, Isolated

Jealous, Joyful, Joyous, Judgmental, Judged, Jaded, Jocular, Jittery, Kind, Keen

Loving, Loved, Love, Lonely, Lackluster, Leery, Lethargic, Listless, Lazy

Mad, Meek, Mean, Miserable, Malevolent, Marvelous, Manipulated, Manipulative, Misunderstood, Mischievous, Mopey, Melodramatic, Moody, Melancholy, Manic, Moved,

Nice, Naughty, Nasty, Nervous, Neglected, Neglectful, Needy, Needed, Naïve, Nonchalant, Nonplussed, Numb

Overpowered, Overjoyed, Obedient, Obsessive, Obsessed, Offended, Outraged, Overloaded, Overwhelmed, Open Overstimulated, Obstinate, Obligated, Optimistic

Panicked, Perseverance, Passive, Peaceful, Prosperous, Powerful, Passionate, Placid, Playful, Pensive, Puzzled, Powerful, Purposed, Powerless, Pleased, Petty, Petulant, Preoccupied, Proud, Prideful, Prickly, Petrified, Pressured,

Relieved, Relaxed, Resentful, Rattled, Refreshed, Resilient, Repulsed, Rational, Reasonable, Reasoned, , Regret, Rebellious, Reluctant, Reassured, Remorseful, Reserved, Rejuvenated, Restless, Rattled

Sad, Strong, Surprised, Silly, Scared, Sorrowful, Self-confident, Serious, Shy, Satisfied, Sensitive, Safe, Stressed, Loved (self), Survival, Stubborn, Sarcastic, Secure, Serene, Sociable, Sympathetic, Startled, Satisfied, Skeptical, Sincere

Thankful, Tearful, Thoughtful, Tranquil, Tolerated, Trusted, Trusting, Trustworthy, Temperamental, Terrified, Timid, Tired, Truthful, Tiresome, Troubled, Torn, Touched, Threatened

Uneasy, Uncertain, Uncomfortable, Unruffled, Unafraid, Useless, Useful, Unimpressed, Unappreciated, Undecided, Unsure, Uptight, Unnerved, Unhappy, Unsteady, Uplifted,

Vivacious, Vain, Vibrant, Violent, Valued, Valuable, Vital, Vexed, Volatile, Vulnerable, Victorious, Victimized, Vacant

Worried, Wary, Weak, Weary, Wistful, Wishful, Willful, Willing, Woeful, Weepy, Whiny, Worn, Whimsical, Warm, Witty, Withdrawn, Worthless, Wronged, Wasted, Worldly

Youthful, Yielding, Yearning

Zany, Zealous, Zestful

Made in the USA
Middletown, DE
05 September 2022